ADHD
Handbook
for Families

A Guide to
Communicating
with Professionals

· · · · · · · · · · · · · · · · · · · ·

Paul L. Weingartner

Child & Family Press • Washington, DC

CWLA Press is an imprint of the Child Welfare League of America. The Child Welfare League of America (CWLA), the nation's oldest and largest membership-based child welfare organization, is committed to engaging all Americans in promoting the well-being of children and protecting every child from harm.

CHILD WELFARE LEAGUE OF AMERICA, INC.
440 First Street, NW, Third Floor, Washington, DC 20001-2085
E-mail: books@cwla.org

CURRENT PRINTING (last digit)
10 9 8 7 6 5 4 3 2

Cover design by Jennifer R. Geanakos
Photo credits: Front cover, second from top, Jan Totty, Athens, GA; fifth from top, David Burgevin, Alexandria, VA; middle bottom, David Burgevin; back cover, third from top, Jan Totty; all others CWLA staff or stock photos

Printed in the United States of America

ISBN # 0–87868-750-5

Library of Congress Cataloging-in-Publication Data

Weingartner, Paul L.
    ADHD handbook for families   :   a guide to communicating with
    professionals / Paul L. Weingartner
        p.   cm.
    Includes bibliographical references
    ISBN 0-87868-750-5 (alk. paper)
    1. Attention-deficit hyperactivity disorder--Treatment.
    2. Attention-deficit disordered children.   3. Behavior disorders in
    children--Treatment.   I. Title
    RJ506.H9W436   1999   98-54949
    618.92'8589--dc21

THIS BOOK IS DEDICATED TO MY WIFE,
Adele (Mueller) Weingartner,
who suggested that I write it,
encouraged me during the process, and
who took on most of the household duties
to give me the time to do so.
As people keep reminding me, I married well.

Contents

Introduction

THINK BACK TO your early school days. You probably knew a boy like me. He was late to school a lot, and his clothes were usually messy, his shirt tails hanging out. He seemed to have trouble keeping his books and papers organized and often lost the workbook pages that he needed to complete. He interrupted the teacher, sometimes blurting out things that had nothing to do with what was going on in the classroom. He had to ask for directions over and over again. He fidgeted all day long and wouldn't stay in his seat. Maybe you thought he was stupid or retarded, and that he belonged in that class with "those other" students. Maybe you thought he was lazy or had a discipline problem. Mostly you thought that he was a real nuisance in the classroom.

Well, I wasn't lazy or retarded or acting out to get attention. I had— and still have—attention-deficit/hyperactivity disorder (ADHD). Highly technical research [Sieg et al. 1995; Halperin et al. 1997; Castellanos et al. 1996; Filipek et al. 1997] reports that, in people with ADHD, regions of the brain are slightly, but distinctly impaired. As a result, these regions do not function as well as "normal" regions. Wender [1997] puts it succinctly: "In most cases, ADHD is genetically transmitted and mediated by decreased dopaminergic activity in the brain."

What does this mean for identification, treatment, attitudes, and expectations about this disorder? The pivotal understanding that ADHD is a **neurobiological** disorder both elicits empathy and dismisses the biases that can cause harm.

Let me illustrate this more specifically. If a typically developing child has an impulse to grab a piece of expensive stemware in a crystal store, he usually has a fraction of a second, between that impulse and actually grabbing it, to run through a list of possible consequences. If this list contains some memory of real trouble when such an action was carried out in the past, that memory may inhibit the impulse. The child may actually override the desire to grab that inviting glass. If the region of the brain that produces that list of consequences is impaired or underactive, however, the child is less likely to inhibit some behaviors properly. The result is all too familiar to parents of children with ADHD.

Quay describes this process as an "underresponsive behavioral inhibitory system" [1997, p. 12]. For children with this disorder, there is no adequate loop of thinking things through before they jump into action or blurt out something—typical impulsive behaviors.

The impairment in brain function may be slight, which causes people with ADHD to present symptoms inconsistently. Think about the remote control on your television set. When the batteries get low, they do not stop working suddenly. Sometimes they work normally, and sometimes you have to push the button over and over again before the battery sends enough current to change the channel. You get some warning that the batteries are going dead, but you may continue to use the remote for a day or two until you have time to buy more.

During that day or two, you live with the frustration of the remote sometimes working perfectly and sometimes not working at all. You have no warning. It is not predictable. A friend may call you and urge you to turn to a certain channel quickly because something important is on. You push the buttons but nothing happens. As the person on the phone rushes you to change the channel, you shake the remote control, push some other buttons desperately, and, just then, the battery delivers enough power to change to another channel that you do not really want.

This is something like a teacher asking a student with ADHD to answer a question, and the student cannot remember one or more of the critical elements necessary to answer the question. The student's anxiety goes up as he attempts to answer the teacher's question, and he gropes around to find clues to answer the question. He makes a wild guess—but the class laughs at him, because his answer is far off the subject. The irretrievable pieces of the answer were not available for the student, because of the slight underactivity of the brain for that function.

ADHD is a neurobiological disorder. Understanding that a part of the brain is impaired and underactive strengthens the professional opinion that people do not outgrow ADHD. Barkley et al. [1990] found that when identification criteria were rigorously followed in assessing children with ADHD, more than 80% of them continued to be identified as ADHD when they were adolescents. Fisher developed criteria that are considered appropriate for adults. He reported that "68% of hyperactive subjects could be seen as showing persistence of ADHD" [Fisher 1997, p. 9].

Roy-Byrne [1997] and colleagues also point out the great challenges in selecting appropriate criteria and instruments for making an appropriate assessment with adults, and noted: "This is probably a reflection of a disorder that is in continued need of refinement, and a testimony to the many pitfalls ... that can make a diagnosis of ADHD in adults extremely difficult."

For this reason, appropriate identification must include information about the symptoms being present for the person's lifetime. Clearly, different settings have different demands upon attention, so a person will not have the same frustrations in all settings. The influence of expectations also varies from one setting to another. Since ADHD is a neurobiological disorder, a person with ADHD does not get along just fine for the first few years of school and suddenly "come down with an attention deficit" in the fourth grade.

With some people, ADHD symptoms present themselves inconsistently. Caregivers have seen the student succeed on some occasions, and that is why they believe that a student's problems are a failure of will, to some extent. They form the opinion that if the student were only more motivated, he would be able to perform all the time.

When the student digs down and does override his symptoms for a short while, this is a tremendous achievement, not a haphazard effort. Ironically, the very effort that is producing this inconsistent result is also producing the evidence to those around him, who say, "He could do it if he only wanted to. I've seen him do it before." It does not take long for the student to get frustrated with this and give up in a whirl of confusion about why this is happening to him.

I wrote this book to change attitudes about ADHD. When I present information about the neurobiological nature of ADHD to teachers, I see a clear change on their faces. Embattled teachers sometimes come to workshops on ADHD with a look of cold skepticism at first. When I inform them otherwise, they no longer see the student as someone who is trying to beat the system. (Who would say this sort of thing about cerebral palsy or myopia?) With this understanding, too, teachers will shift from saying, "Just try harder," to "What can we do that works?"

If we accept that this disorder presents real, if subtle, learning challenges, then we will want to know what *does* work. What can the various people in the student's environments—teachers, parents, siblings, classmates—do to increase the likelihood of success?

This book is designed to help. Chapters One through Three provide background information on ADHD: what it feels like, why it's difficult to identify, and how our attitudes about ADHD affect our understanding of the disorder.

Because ADHD is a neurobiological disorder, we can observe the effects it has on our child and record our observations. This process, described in Chapters Four and Five, will be critical in working with a treatment professional on a successful intervention. Chapter Six suggests resources you can use to find the appropriate person to help. Chapters Seven and Eight describe medical and psychosocial interventions.

Chapters Nine through Twelve offer steps for "following-up" on intervention. This follow-up includes further observing and recording, as well as developing behavior modification plans and strategies. Again, this process will assist you in working with a treatment professional, teachers, and other members of the family.

Chapters Thirteen through Fifteen include additional information for you to use, and my own account of how I applied the processes of observing, recording, and modifying my behavior.

Empathy builds the bonds of a relationship that fuels the inventiveness to find ways toward success that did not exist before. I hope this book will inform families and professionals about methods and strategies for working with children with ADHD.

CHAPTER ONE

. . . .

How It Feels to Have ADHD

TRUDGING YOUR WAY through life with attention-deficit/hyperactivity disorder (ADHD)* is hard work. Margaret Stolowitz makes that graphically clear for us with her personal story. She writes, "My school life was awful from the beginning to the bitter end ... and even today I remember the awful feelings of failure and frustrations" [Stolowitz 1997, p. 10]. Many people, however, do not appreciate your efforts—and you often do not appreciate yourself [Sabian 1995]. Having ADHD is like punching through a wet paper bag only to find that outside that bag is a larger wet paper bag that will also need to be punched through. Sometimes you honestly think you are making progress, but you are getting exhausted, while others seem to be walking effortlessly through the bags as if they were only shimmering veils of light.

---

* The standard features of ADHD are spelled out in the *Diagnostic and Statistical Manual of Mental Disorders* (4th ed.) published by the American Psychiatric Association [1994]. This is often referred to as the DSM-IV. Currently there are four subtypes of attention-deficit disorder: Attention-Deficit/Hyperactivity Disorder Predominantly Hyperactive-Impulsive Type (314.01), Attention-Deficit/Hyperactivity Disorder Predominantly Inattentive Type (314.00), Attention-Deficit/Hyperactivity Disorder Com-

This book is a message from one who has not only suffered with the thousand doubts and frustrations of ADHD, but has gone on to be trained, licensed, and then have professionally helped thousands of individuals who also have this disorder.

When conducting workshops on ADHD, I have found it helpful to start by making people aware of what it is like to live with ADHD. Imagine that you are sitting in the room outside a courtroom. Imagine that you are guilty, and when they call you into the courtroom, you will be prosecuted, have to pay a huge fine, and will likely serve a lengthy sentence in jail.

Now imagine that there is a delay. While you are sitting there, you will be agitated. You will get up and get a drink of water at the fountain. You will sit down. You will get up and get another drink of water. You will sit down again. A family member sitting next to you may be trying to talk to you about some upcoming family function.

That family member will become frustrated with you, because you do not appear to care at all about what she is saying. She may even accuse you of not caring enough about the family. In short, you will have all the symptoms of ADHD without having the disorder at all.

A person in such a situation may respond by getting angry and point out how unfair it is to be expected to think about family plans when he or she is in such a difficult situation. A person with ADHD, particularly a young person, will more likely assume that the blame lies with himself. He will feel bad that he, once again, is doing something wrong. He is, again, making someone angry with him. He will sink into de-

---

bined type (314.01), and Attention-Deficit/Hyperactivity Disorder Not Otherwise Specified (314.9). The numbers in parentheses are the diagnostic codes. The criteria for these subtypes can be found in the DSM-IV, but they are generally based upon observations of inattention, distractibility, and difficulty with organization and management. (Hyperactivity is a physical overactivity that is pronounced, even when the individual's age is taken into consideration.) In this book, I use the acronym ADHD to indicate attention-deficit disorder with and without hyperactivity.

spair at how he seems to keep causing people around him so much frustration, but he doesn't know why.

Trying to salvage the situation, he may make some halting response about plans that will only further infuriate the family member, because it will betray that he has missed the last 16 things she has said. He chides himself for trying at all. Hasn't he learned before not to try?

Now picture a student just as distracted sitting in a classroom being taught regrouping for addition in mathematics. Through some extreme exertion of effort, he grasps the more basic concept of addition without regrouping. He wants to celebrate. He wants to finally have the feeling that he has accomplished something, but the rest of the class had that feeling a few weeks ago and they are now learning to regroup, or carry a numeral over to the next higher place value and add that column.

His brief hope of feeling joy is crushed under the realization that there is another whole package of things to be learned. He does not have the energy to stay with the explanation much longer, and he sinks into his distractions, waiting with fear instead of joy for the inevitable tongue lashing that is coming his way when he is called upon to answer.

These swings of joy and fear exhaust him, causing him anxiety and confusion, and further reinforce his convictions that there is something wrong with him, but since none of these big people around him seem to know what to do, it must be something he is failing to do himself.

So now he gets to go out on the playground. He is standing there waiting to be invited to join in a group activity, but he is the odd-man-out because the teacher has been yelling at him. He has been marked and is subtly shunned. A big red rubber ball is coming at his head. Someone he doesn't see is yelling to duck, but he does not hear the warning. Then, a ringing sort of clap goes through his ear and mind as the ball hits him in the head and bounces off in another direction. The other children on the playground laugh at him and ask him if he is deaf. Since he can hear those questions, he knows that he can hear clearly. He just does not know what is wrong.

Then he goes home, and his father wants him to help carry something out of the garage. He is a big boy for his age, so he guardedly allows himself a little pride that he can be of some help to his father. Here, at last, might be a chance for some joy, some accomplishment. He and his father walk up to a table saw. His father tells him not to lift it by the round poles that the top slides back and forth on, because that would bend the poles. While the father is telling him this, however, he has already seen them, and concluded that they are shaped to be the perfect things to grab because they have no sharp edges. This mental analysis of their ideal properties for being handles has so engaged his mind that he did not perceive his father telling him not to use them.

He innocently reaches out for them and his father screams at him not to touch those. The father then asks him if he heard the instructions not to touch them. It was recent enough that he does have an awareness of those instructions but they had not worked their way to his consciousness until his father asked about them. On top of all his other problems, he now has a moral dilemma. Does he admit to his father that he heard it and invite a torrent of invective, or does he lie about it—in which case his father will not believe it anyway and list all the things he does seem to be able to hear. This will spark angry speculation in his father about what is really going on—speculation that is quite unlikely to include undifferentiated ADHD.

Then it will happen. His father, who has voiced concerns to other family members that he may be retarded, will call him that name that is worse than all other names. It is not worse for the name itself. It is worse because it comes from the one person in the world whom he has admired the most in his first six or seven years of life. His father will call him, "Tin Ear."

This is an example of ADHD that does not have hyperactivity with it. While ADHD with hyperactivity has more dramatic, visible symptoms, the subtype *without* hyperactivity has been more often overlooked and misunderstood. The need for sympathetic help and planning should be obvious.

There is a wide difference of opinion about the lifespan of ADHD, which can be identified at any time during a person's development. If the identification is delayed, however, the individual's emotional health will certainly suffer [Ratley et al. 1997]. Living with the consequences of ADHD usually causes individuals to assume blame and to lower their opinion of their self-worth both as a student and as an individual [Anderson et al. 1989; Brooks 1994].

A person's assessment of himself should be as accurate as possible. Being coached into an assessment of yourself that is higher than your abilities support, ultimately, will cause problems. Students with ADHD, however, tend to form harmful beliefs about themselves as learners, underestimating their abilities because of their frustrating experiences.

CHAPTER TWO

. . . .

What Makes ADHD So Difficult to Identify?

ATTENTION-DEFICIT/HYPERACTIVITY DISORDER (ADHD) is a complex disorder that is often quite difficult to recognize. Even though this disorder has been researched and treated for decades, professionals who work with children disagree that this disorder even exists. This disagreement causes great frustration to the children and parents who come to these professionals seeking help and intervention.

ADHD is a neurological disorder, and this information changes many of our ideas about identification. During professional seminars, researchers present slides of brain images made from either computer-enhanced electroencephalographies (EEGs), magnetic resonance imaging, or blood flow, using rediopharmaceuticals in a process called single photon emission tomography (SPECT). These slides show clear but subtle differences in many cases. When shown to clinicians, the first question is inevitably, "Can this distinction be used as a hard diagnostic tool?" So far, the answer remains, "No." Levy [1994] concludes that efforts to develop a diagnostic tool are well spent, but it is premature to expect effective tools for identification.

The major obstacle to recognition is that, while ADHD is a neuro-biological disability, it has no hard diagnostic markers. You cannot, yet, wire a person up to an electronic machine and take readings where there is an absolute score above which you have ADHD and below which you clearly do not. So while it is a neurobiological disorder, it still has a subjective diagnosis.

Most people working in the field believe ADHD has a neurobiological basis that is not "curable" but that will remain a lifelong feature of the personality. They believe that ADHD is caused by a slight impairment to a portion of the brain. A widely held view [Barkley 1997b] is that this impairment is in the portion of the brain that performs such executive functions as working memory; internalization of speech (self-talk); self-regulation of affect, motivation, and arousal; and reconstitution (the ability to take apart and reconstruct behavioral sequences).

One reason for the difficulty in identifying ADHD is that ADHD symptoms do not present themselves consistently. Another is that children who have ADHD frequently have other behavior problems that cause adjustment challenges in schools or with authority figures. At one time, people thought about this in an "either/or" way. Either a student had ADHD or he had oppositional defiant disorder. She either had ADHD, or she had adjustment disorder with anxious mood.

Frequently students have both, and caregivers and professionals need to respond to both with appropriate intervention plans. Much personal history and information is required to decide whether one or more conditions exist. It is critical to take into account the following challenges to recognition when examining the various histories.

Inconsistent Symptoms

There are no symptoms that are unique to ADHD. The behaviors observed in ADHD are also seen in many affective, personality, adjustment, and behavioral disorders.

Students with ADHD do not always show the same degree of impairment. Tannock states that "the situational variability of symptom expression may lead some clinicians to conclude that a child does not have ADHD because the symptoms are not sufficiently persistent or pervasive" [1997, p. 3]. What this means is that, at the same time a professional may be assessing the presence of a disorder, the child is probably trying to suppress the symptoms. The child has been developing strategies for coping with the symptoms or disguising them. The success of those strategies depends upon a number of factors: rest, support, nutrition, motivation, a sense of caring, and others.

With sufficient motivation, people with ADHD can dig deeply inside themselves and find the power to stay focused for longer than they usually do. Unfortunately, the individual will not be able to sustain this level of attention for long. It may be long enough, however, to cause a person working with him to form the opinion, so often heard in this area: "He can do it when he wants to."

This inconsistent presentation of symptoms has confused people about the nature of ADHD. Ironically, the individual's efforts to overcome the symptoms work against more rapid identification of the disorder.

Adjustment Problems

Picture a toddler sitting in a playroom with just one adult with her. Imagine her putting together a large, colorful, wooden puzzle designed for her age. If she were taking three times the normal time it takes to put the puzzle together and was spending the other time looking around and watching the adult, the adult might not be concerned at all. The adult might even be flattered by the child's attention.

Now picture the same toddler as a first grader in a classroom of 25 other students. Suppose that she were asked to connect some matching pictures on a page with a pencil line. If she took three times as long as the other students because she was looking around, particularly at the teacher, she would probably receive some prompting to "get to work." Over time, other students would probably note her relative "slowness" in getting the job done. Worse yet, she might draw some conclusions about her own skills, due to these delays and comments. She might look for ways to avoid this "threat," which might cause further prompting and further unwanted attention from teachers and other students.

Over time, this process causes her to believe negative things about herself as a learner and to either avoid difficult situations or act out to distract from her problems. More than just coping with the new classroom lessons, she also has to cope with these challenges to her identity, reputation, and the fears that her parents might not be pleased.

Before ADHD can be identified, then, some children develop another disorder: oppositional defiant disorder. The child has created an unfortunate social reputation and now must fight battles on several fronts at once. In some cases, adults recognize the oppositional defiant disorder first and begin disciplinary measures that never acknowledge the underlying ADHD.

If everyone sent to the assistant principal's office for not completing work were evaluated for ADHD, what might the results be? Romeo [1996] reported that 41% of a sample of maximum security inmates were either treated or assessed for childhood ADHD. Satterfield and Schell [1997] report an increased risk for later criminality in children with hyperactivity and conduct problems. We can only speculate about how many of today's serious offenders might have been given a better chance in life if we had known more about ADHD a generation or two ago.

Adjustment problems do not disappear once a proper diagnosis has been found. Impulsiveness, hyperactivity, or inattention continue to be a lifelong feature for these individuals. Even when medication is prescribed and works successfully, the student still has adjustment concerns. Imagine sitting among all your friends in school listening to a lecture about how bad "drugs" are for you and then needing to run to the office at lunch to take your pill. Many students have difficulty with this. Some refuse to cooperate with this regimen, which makes other medical options necessary. The students who do cooperate with this regimen, however, often find that they have to try to explain why they go to the office, and what they do there.

Sometimes they run into an influential adult in their lives who tells them that they do not really need this medication and they have to work through the whole matter again.

It would be bad enough if this were going on all by itself, but keep in mind that these adjustment problems are piled on top of a student who is already trying to remember assignments, learn regrouping in math, bring home the parent signature form for something, write an outline by Thursday, find a best friend at lunch, avoid going down one hall where he might get in a fight, and take an apple to that teacher who does not really like him.

In short, school is a cauldron of intellectual, social, and emotional challenges. ADHD only multiplies these challenges. Some students can slug their way through successfully just by pure grit, some get lucky and get school staff who understand and are flexible, and some get destroyed.

CHAPTER THREE

· ·

How Expectations Affect Understanding

UNDERSTANDING THE neurobiological basis of attention-deficit/hyperactivity disorder (ADHD) makes it clear that there will be no magic time in the future when the child will get tired of this behavior and come around to doing better. It is not something he will likely outgrow. It is not something that will go away when someone breaks his strong will. This is a lifelong feature of this individual and has certain advantages and disadvantages. Understand these and expect to deal with them on a daily basis—but do not expect them to go away. Time spent wishing or waiting for them to go away is time wasted.

Adjusting our expectations to fit reality is one of the surest ways to reduce frustration. Most of the major conflicts between people have to do with one person holding expectations for another that he should have known were unrealistic in advance. This is not to say that we should just drop our expectations. Why write a book to cope and overcome a disorder if you recommended dropping all expectations? Instead, we should get the expectations accurate, focused, and reasonable.

The Power of Expectations

There is a folk story about some psychological "research" that was done decades ago to demonstrate how powerfully people can communicate their expectations without words. I doubt that the research was ever done, or if so, I doubt that it was ever replicated or we would all be more familiar with it. I relate it here because I think it strikes a chord we all understand, even if we do not have robust scientific research to support it.

The legend goes that there were 300 people in a study. One hundred—let us call them group A—were told that they were each to go into a room and wait and someone would come in and give them a $10 bill. One hundred others—group B—were told that they were to go into the same rooms and wait and someone would come into the room and give them a $1 bill. One hundred others—group C—were given a $10 bill and a $1 bill and told to go into a room where there would be two people. They were to give the $10 bill to one and the $1 bill to the other and they were not to talk to anyone or communicate in any way to find out who was to receive which bill.

According to legend, group C gave out the correct denomination of bills 80% of the time. Since this was so much higher than the expected 50%, researchers concluded that people have a way of communicating their expectations in nonverbal, unknown ways. That is, the person expecting the $10 bill somehow communicated the fact that he was expecting to receive a $10 bill. And similarly for the $1 bill person.

This legend reminds us of the "self-fulfilling prophecy" concept, which is the same thing. If people *expect* to have problems, they can unwittingly behave in ways that will cause those problems. (Understanding this, and becoming aware of how difficult it is for us to see these behaviors in ourselves is what much of counseling is about.)

Expectations of Different Settings

ADHD is dynamically related to its environment. Most disorders are, of course, but with ADHD, this is especially true. There can be times and places when the symptoms of an ADHD are an asset, not a liability. In fact, Jensen and colleagues [1997] suggest that some specific pathogenic environments may actually cause this disorder and that certain environments influence brain development in young children. This research is not referring to habits formed around video game use, but actual organic brain development altered in the early years before children begin playing with video games.

If the individual were living among the nomadic tribes of northern Africa, or the rain forests of Brazil, he would be king of the hill. In these dangerous environments, it is valuable to be vigilant and aware of every movement. To be constantly alert to all movement around you, every stir in the tall grass, could give you the earliest warning of a tiger or a boa constrictor ready to attack. It is easy to see how this could be a matter of life and death.

You don't even have to go to a foreign land. If a student with ADHD works in a retail shop waiting on customers, he may never anger a customer by not knowing who came in second, third, and so on. He would be aware of every customer in the store and who should be waited on next. He would also be alert to who is loitering too long around small expensive merchandise. He might move to that customer to prevent shoplifting. Hypervigilence to all environmental stimuli will prove to be a genuine asset in this environment.

In a large classroom where students are expected to remain seated quietly for hours, working independently among 30 other students, however, this same alertness to every movement in the environment presents a real challenge.

Not only are there differences in settings, but Carlson and others [1997] identify differences between boys and girls with ADHD and oppositional defiant disorder. So ADHD is a complex set of symptoms that do not exist alone, but interact with places and people across time.

Teacher Expectations

Some teachers have more behavior problems with students through the years than others. Any given year can present a class with a high number of unruly students, but over the years this should balance out. Still, some teachers seem to have more problems year after year.

This is so true that I can walk through any public elementary school in the summer with no teachers or students around and tell you which teachers have more problems. Theirs are the classrooms with all the vandalism. Their desks have more carvings in the wood. Their pencil sharpener has been destroyed. Their globe has pock marks. Their dictionaries have many pages torn out.

These teachers are usually rigid, inflexible, uptight, hostile, impatient, sarcastic, and unhappy themselves. They may be strict and insufficiently communicative. They may be capricious, subject to change without believing that they have an obligation to explain the change or to provide the necessary coaching and rehearsing to help children with ADHD with the change.

Teachers' expectations play a big role. If their expectations are unrealistic and they want all children to sit squarely in the middle of their desk with their feet flat on the floor under their desk and work for hours without a sound, they are in for frustration. If they believe that they can hand out six pages or worksheets at the beginning of the day, explain them all at one time, and expect the students to remember the explanations, and work dutifully on them one by one as they go down through the stack, they are on a collision course with at least 5% of their students each and every year.

One of my sons had a wonderful elementary school teacher who had four sons of her own. She seemed to have an expectation that boys will be unruly and even get in little pushing fights now and then. None of this bothered her. She was able to ignore much of this. As a result there was essentially no tension in her classroom. My son loved her. Everyone loved her.

We can, however, expect a certain common level of training. Courses in instructional methods, in human development, and individual differences, tend to narrow the possible differences in teaching styles that exist between teachers. With parents, this is all different.

Parent Expectations

It has been lamented everywhere that you cannot get a driver's license without taking classes and passing tests, but there are no such effective road blocks to being a parent. The result is a wide range of diversity among parents.

In the same classroom you may have the son of the local municipal court judge and the daughter of an antigovernment survivalist. You may have a student who is one of 12 siblings and a student who is an only child.

You may have parents who have a gifted child but who have no particular educational ambitions for their child, and a demanding, pushy parent of a student with low ability.

More confusing, you may have parents who are overconfident about their parenting methods and see no need for help as they mishandle their children, and you may have parents who are totally without faith in their parenting methods and who listen to and experiment with all parenting advice indiscriminately. (I'm not sure which is more harmful to the children.)

It seems intuitive that parents' methods and skills play an influential part in their child's overall presentation of symptoms, even if ADHD is essentially a neurobiological disorder. This was also the conclusion of Hinshaw in an interesting examination of just these ideas when he writes,

"Parenting interventions that emphasize positive interchange, clear limits for misbehavior, and parenting anger control thus appear critical for high-risk populations that include youth with ADHD" [1997, p. 8].

Parents, like teachers, can communicate expectations that will influence their child's behavior. Some parents seem to roll with parenting challenges calmly with little anxiety. Some parents seem to interpret every twitch as an early warning sign and worry their children into problems. Certainly parents need judgment to know when and how to act, and what to ignore. We do not automatically "inherit" this judgment—it has to be learned.

CHAPTER FOUR

. . . .

Diagnosis: Collecting Information

ATTENTION-DEFICIT/HYPERACTIVITY DISORDER (ADHD) has become almost a fad disorder in recent years. People seem quick to disclose that they have the disorder, even if sometimes they are only joking. As a result, several professional journals have published cautions to guard against overdiagnosis [Murphy 1994], and professionals have used methods to diagnose this disorder that vary widely in their thoroughness and, therefore, their accuracy.

For example, it is not "best practice" for a clinician to simply ask a child to draw a picture and, if the child can do it with little or no wiggling, refuse to consider the possibility of ADHD. This, unfortunately, was a real experience that occurred just months before I wrote this book. I met some parents who had taken a report that carefully documented the presence of ADHD based upon all the considerations covered in this chapter. Their clinician dismissed the matter in the above manner. While this experience is relatively rare, it does still happen. It is extremely frustrating, and causes parents to wonder what to do next.

One effective way to ensure that your concerns will be seriously considered is to gather information that illustrates the observations you are making about your child. Quantifiable examples are quite valuable to professionals when they begin assessing your child for ADHD. But where do you go to gather such "data"?

Multiple Settings

There are at least three places to look for information when making the diagnosis of ADHD: the home, the school, and the clinical assessment. For many reasons, children behave differently from setting to setting. For milder instances, and cases where hyperactivity is not present, the disorder may be first noticed only in the more rigid structure of a classroom environment. The classroom, demanding children to wait their turn and stand in line, may be the first place the child is expected to do that. Of course, a parent may have made similar requests but when the child was unable to perform them, most parents adjusted and took care of the child's demands immediately. A classroom teacher is not always able to do that.

For this reason, the ideal clinical assessment utilizes information from both the home and classroom. Personal interviews with persons in these settings and direct observation are ideal; however, sometimes questionnaires may be used when the personal approach is not possible. When the assessment concerns an adult, it is helpful to get information from parents who can remember childhood behaviors.

Complete Histories

Goldstein draws upon 25 years of experience working with ADHD and urges us to listen to caregivers, saying, "History is our best ally for initial case formulation and the generation of diagnostic hypotheses" [1997, p. 5].

Accuracy is further enhanced if these sources can offer data covering as much of the student's history as possible. For example, it is one matter if a fourth grader has been reported to have had attention-span concerns every year of his or her schooling. It is another matter if a fourth grader has earned superior ratings in school from preschool through the third grade and has only begun having attention-span difficulties in the fourth grade.

It is not important that data from these three sources agree. It is important that they are weighed, balanced, and reconciled in the final opinion. Sometimes one of these sources will have a compelling private agenda to have the child diagnosed or not diagnosed. Information from that source may be biased, contrived, or forced, whether intentionally or not. This is, itself, important information, but obviously not conclusive information. Some decision-making process is needed that will consider all these data against what is known about typical human development. The proper diagnosis is not simply a mathematical addition of equally weighted indicators from these three sources where the sum of more than a certain number confirms the diagnosis.

Many efforts have been made to improve the efficiency and accuracy of measures to either screen [Bussin et al. 1998] or evaluate [Anastopoulos et al. 1995] people for ADHD with mixed results. There are still no hard markers defining absolutely the presence of ADHD.

The ideal approach, then, is a coordinated investigation using a health care provider, a school psychologist, all involved teachers, and all involved primary caregivers with parenting responsibilities. Any one or more of those sources can have the initial suspicion that ADHD exists. These sources may gather whatever part of the data they can, and call the other members of this ideal team together. The professional assuming the responsibility for pulling all these data together is typically either the school psychologist or the health care provider. Whoever initiates the collection of data, it is likely that all parties will be communicating with each other, and sometimes, the exchange is frequent.

The Collectors' Responsibilities

PARENTS

Parents have the opportunity to observe the student in the widest ranges of settings—that may surprise most parents. Frequently, parents tend to minimize their contribution to the assessment. They have, by far, the richest pool of information to bring to the assessment process. Most excellent parents are too emotionally involved—as they should be—to objectively view the information they possess, and this information is most useful when subjected to objective professional analysis. This analysis should be done deliberately and in the parents' presence, so that they can correct any assumptions the professionals might be making about the data.

Parents have the opportunity to observe the student in public settings (restaurants, theaters, and stores); private settings (bathing, toileting, and dressing); with family, friends, and strangers; during pleasant activities (video games, television, and parties); and during unpleasant activities (chores, homework, and grooming).

A good behavior checklist or interview will be sure to cover each of these situations and more.* We can all understand how a student might behave differently in public places and in private places, or when just among family or when guests are present. All this information is helpful in taking an account of the student's behavior.

Parents will also have valuable information about other environmental features that may have a bearing on the student's behavior. It is significant if a family recently moved from a larger home to a small one. It is helpful to know whether there are conflicts with one or more members of the immediate family, or others who may come in and out of the home.

Many parents are open enough to volunteer that other members of the family have the same behaviors they see in their child. Frequently one parent will say that he or she had similar problems in school. Other parents may not have this information, as in the case of some adoptions where nothing is known of the family history.

---

* For good examples of behavioral checklists, see R. A. Barkley. (1997). *Defiant Children: A Clinician's manual for assessment and parent training* (2nd ed.). New York: Guilford Press.

Some parents have all this information carefully charted and documented. Others seem to be less observant of these matters.

TEACHERS

Teachers also have a wealth of information about the individual student, and they also have a built-in norm group in the classroom with which to compare the student in question. If the teacher has had much classroom experience, this norm group expands accordingly. (Merrell and Wolfe [1998] have reported on the relationship between teacher-related social skills and ADHD characteristics in children.)

Teachers also see the student in a wide range of settings. They observe the student in one-on-one teaching experiences, in small groups or pairs, in large class groupings, auditoriums, moving through hallways, on playgrounds, gymnasiums, cafeterias, buses, etc.

A good rating form will sample all these situations as well. This information will be valuable when interventions are discussed. Wolraich and others report on the effectiveness of one such rating form:

> The Vanderbilt AD/HD Diagnostic Teachers Rating Scale is a relatively easy rating scale to complete that provides DSM-IV-specific information relating to AD/HD. It also provides screening information relating to oppositional-defiant/conduct, and anxiety/depressive disorders. Its ease of completion is demonstrated by the fact that a large number of teachers completed the scale for the children in their classes for two consecutive years." [Wolraich et al. 1998, p. 149]

Because a teacher usually sees so many students of the same age, and in the same settings, the teacher can provide valuable information about the degree to which the behavior of the student in question varies from his peers. Some classroom observation forms even require the observer to rate the "target" student (the one being evaluated) and one "control" student (a fellow student not suspected of ADHD) both on the same form to ensure that this comparison is done.

Some teachers, like some parents, are highly organized and can communicate these matters objectively. Others are more instantly accommodating and do not even realize how much they are automatically adjusting to their individual students' needs. In addition, teachers vary widely in their knowledge of these disorders.

SCHOOL PSYCHOLOGISTS

The school psychologist is perhaps the best placed professional for this area of concern. At the fulcrum of two huge bodies of research, psychology and education, the school psychologist is well positioned to orchestrate both diagnosis and treatment.

The school psychologist can gather the behavior checklists used to sample the various environments: home, school, day care, latch key programs, etc. The school psychologist also has experience with a large number of other students of the same age to have an opinion of the degree to which the behavior of the student in question differs from the general population.

The primary contribution of the school psychologist is to administer individual tests to gather information about intelligence, academic achievement, adaptive behavior, and personality/emotional development. These data help in sorting out the possible causes for the behaviors in question.

For example, a student may appear quite agitated, off-task, and distracted if he is placed in an algebra class when he has poor arithmetic skills. A teacher might consider the student disruptive and easily distracted, not able to hand in much homework, and what homework is turned in may be messy, with little work done. Having valid information about this student's math achievement levels will help prevent this error in judgment. Keep in mind that a student can still have both ADHD and low math achievement levels, but, if he has low math achievement levels, the evaluation team will have to see evidence of ADHD in other settings besides the algebra classroom alone.

Another student may appear distracted, off-task, and agitated in school when she is in a near panic of anxiety about violent arguments overheard at home. Perhaps her family is going through difficult times, and she is feeling responsible for the difficulties. Perhaps she is being abused and the others working with her do not know about it yet.

These matters will show up on some part of the testing battery and will have a substantial impact on intervention plans. Some results on personality testing have direct influence on which medications a health provider might consider using. For example, some medications may actually aggravate anxieties or depressions identified on the testing.

HEALTH CARE PROVIDERS

The family doctor, or specialist in children's health, plays a vital part in assessment. Often this individual is the first line of defense. Parents bring up concerns with their health care provider when they see behaviors that they fear are unusual. In some cases, this is long before the school years, making the responsibility for early intervention rest mainly with the doctor.

If a medication is prescribed, it will be this specialist who will make that decision and prescribe it. Doctors have historically used behavior checklists in an effort to measure the frequency and severity of behavior problems before and after a medication is used. (Examples of such behavioral checklists, developed by Abbot Laboratories*, are provided on following pages.) They often try to get these behavior checklists from both the home and the school, if the patient is in school.

Doctors should insist on periodic visits to monitor the patient's response to the medication. They should listen for reports of possible side effects and make other physical examinations to ensure that all is going as expected. Doctors will vary in their comfort in this area. Some

---

* Abbot Laboratories deserves much recognition for putting into doctors' hands such a useful instrument as early as it did. There are now, much later, better instruments to use, but this responsible company was early and aggressive at helping health providers make better judgments if they used this instrument.

Parent's Questionnaire

Name of child _____

Date _____

Please answer all questions. Beside each item, indicate the degree of the problem by a check mark (✓).

	Not at all	Just a little	Pretty much	Very much
1. Picks at things (nails, fingers, hair, clothing)				
2. Sassy to grown-ups				
3. Problems with making or keeping friends				
4. Excitable, impulsive				
5. Wants to run things				
6. Sucks or chews (thumb, clothing, blankets)				
7. Cries easily or often				
8. Carries a chip on his/her shoulder				
9. Daydreams				
10. Difficulty in learning				
11. Restless in the "squirmy" sense				
12. Fearful (of new situations, new people or places, going to school)				
13. Restless, always up and on the go				
14. Destructive				
15. Tells lies or stories that aren't true				
16. Shy				
17. Gets into more trouble than others of the same age				
18. Speaks differently from others of the same age (baby talk, stuttering, hard to understand				
19. Denies mistakes or blames others				
20. Quarrelsome				
21. Pouts and sulks				
22. Steals				
23. Disobedient or obeys, but resentfully				

	Not at all	Just a little	Pretty much	Very much
24. Worries more than others (about being alone, illness, or death)				
25. Fails to finish things				
26. Feelings easily hurt				
27. Bullies others				
28. Unable to stop a repetitive activity				
29. Cruel				
30. Childish or immature (wants help he/she doesn't need, clings, needs constant reassurance)				
31. Distractibility or attention span a problem				
32. Headaches				
33. Mood changes quickly and drastically				
34. Doesn't like or doesn't follow rules or restrictions				
35. Fights constantly				
36. Doesn't get along well with brothers or sisters				
37. Easily frustrated in efforts				
38. Disturbs other children				
39. Basically an unhappy child				
40. Problems with eating (poor appetite, up between bites)				
41. Stomach aches				
42. Problems with sleep (can't fall asleep, up too early, up in the night)				
43. Other aches and pains				
44. Vomiting or nausea				
45. Feels cheated in family circle				
46. Boasts and brags				
47. Lets self be pushed around				
48. Bowel problems (frequently loose, irregular habits, constipation)				

Teacher's Questionnaire

Name of child _____   Grade _____

Please answer all questions. Beside each item, indicate the degree of the problem by a check mark (✓).

	Not at all	Just a little	Pretty much	Very much
1. Restless in the "squirmy" sense				
2. Makes inappropriate noises when he/she shouldn't				
3. Demands must be met immediately				
4. Acts "smart" (impudent or sassy)				
5. Temper outbursts and unpredictable behavior				
6. Overly sensitive to criticism				
7. Distractibility or attention span a problem				
8. Disturbs other children				
9. Daydreams				
10. Pouts and sulks				
11. Mood changes quickly and drastically				
12. Quarrelsome				
13. Submissive attitude toward authority				
14. Restless, always up and "on the go"				
15. Excitable, impulsive				
16. Excessive demands for teacher's attention				
17. Appears to be unaccepted by group				
18. Appears to be easily led by other children				
19. No sense of fair play				
20. Appears to lack leadership				
21. Fails to finish things that he/she starts				
22. Childish and immature				
23. Denies mistakes or blames others				
24. Does not get along well with other children				
25. Uncooperative with classmates				
26. Easily frustrated in efforts				
27. Uncooperative with teacher				
28. Difficulty in learning				

refer parents to specialists. Some ask parents to gather more information for them. Some prefer to handle the matter themselves.

Often parents report that medication contributes a great deal to the relief of symptoms and the improvement of the home climate. There are many dramatic stories to tell here. Perhaps the most rewarding are those of parents who first adamantly refused medication for a year or so. Then, out of frustration, they may have grudgingly tried a medication for the usual 30 days. In some of these stories, the student's reaction to the 30-day trial and continued success with the medication, was so dramatic that the parents deeply regretted not using the medication immediately the first time it was recommended to them. The importance of this part of the intervention picture should be appreciated.

It is important for the family, or the individual, to give the clinician the information they have in a clear way. For that reason, I have created some forms that will be introduced in the next chapter to help in this important step of communicating with professionals.

Chapter Five

. . . .

Diagnosis: Recording Information

You do not have the same burden of reporting expected of you that a professional would have. Still, this book will make you a trained family member. You will find that clearer reporting will help the professional better serve you and your child.

Always speak to professionals with a soft, respectful voice, but carry a big stick. The big stick is information about two categories: what your concerns are specifically and what you know the professional should do. On pages 32 and 33 are sample behavior reporting forms that you may use to ensure that you communicate helpful details to the professional. You will need to use a separate form like this for each of the concerning behaviors. Make a copy of these forms and give them to the professional you select. Take the time to go over them area by area to ensure that he/she does not just put them in the file without carefully reading them. Do not allow an assistant to take them and put them in the file for you. Gently, but firmly, say that you wish to point out many items on these pages personally and then they can be added to the file.

Child Target Behavior Reporting Form

1. What specific behavior is clearly seen?

2. How often does it happen?
   - ❏ 1x/week
   - ❏ 1x/day
   - ❏ 2-5x/day
   - ❏ 6-10x/day
   - ❏ 1x/hour
   - ❏ 2-5x/hour
   - ❏ more

3. How severe is this behavior?
   - ❏ annoying
   - ❏ interrupts things
   - ❏ disrupts everything around
   - ❏ gets into trouble with rules

4. Where does this behavior occur?
   - ❏ home
   - ❏ gym
   - ❏ classroom
   - ❏ cafeteria
   - ❏ bus
   - ❏ individually
   - ❏ car
   - ❏ stores
   - ❏ small group meetings
   - ❏ hallways
   - ❏ offices
   - ❏ playground
   - ❏ restaurants
   - ❏ businesses
   - ❏ other _____

5. Who sees this behavior?
   - ❏ mom
   - ❏ dad
   - ❏ teacher
   - ❏ coaches
   - ❏ tutors
   - ❏ aides
   - ❏ counselors
   - ❏ principal
   - ❏ specialists
   - ❏ neighbors
   - ❏ everyone

6. How long has this behavior existed?
   - ❏ all life
   - ❏ 3 yrs on
   - ❏ 5 yrs on
   - ❏ just started
   - ❏ specific years _____

7. What have you tried to stop this behavior?

8. What seems to work in reducing this behavior at least some of the time?

Adult Target Behavior Reporting Form

1. What specific behavior is clearly seen?

2. How often does it happen?
   - ❏ 1x/week
   - ❏ 1x/day
   - ❏ 2-5x/day
   - ❏ 6-10x/day
   - ❏ 1x/hour
   - ❏ 2-5x/hour
   - ❏ more

3. How severe is this behavior?
   - ❏ annoying
   - ❏ interrupts things
   - ❏ disrupts everything around
   - ❏ gets into trouble with rules

4. Where does this behavior occur?
   - ❏ home
   - ❏ gym
   - ❏ classroom
   - ❏ cafeteria
   - ❏ bus
   - ❏ individually
   - ❏ car
   - ❏ stores
   - ❏ small group meetings
   - ❏ hallways
   - ❏ offices
   - ❏ playground
   - ❏ restaurants
   - ❏ businesses
   - ❏ other _____

5. Who sees this behavior?
   - ❏ spouse
   - ❏ mom
   - ❏ dad
   - ❏ siblings
   - ❏ relatives
   - ❏ supervisors
   - ❏ co-workers
   - ❏ specialists
   - ❏ children
   - ❏ neighbors
   - ❏ everyone

6. How long has this behavior existed?
   - ❏ all life
   - ❏ 3 yrs on
   - ❏ 5 yrs on
   - ❏ just started
   - ❏ specific years _____

7. What have you tried to stop this behavior?

8. What seems to work in reducing this behavior at least some of the time?

These forms are not busy work. There are details important to history and diagnosis on them that you will recognize from the first four chapters of this book.

Do not worry if your reporting on these forms proves to be less than precise. You are giving the professional your impressions in as clear and careful a way as possible. These documents do not replace nationally normed behavior rating forms, or other evaluation instruments that the professional will elect to use to further pursue the concerns. These documents will suggest to the professional that you have not dropped in on a whim or because you have just seen or read something about attention-deficit/hyperactivity disorder (ADHD). It will convey that you have considered many of the matters about frequency, severity, pervasiveness, and longevity that are important to consider in this area.

When a professional receives information in this format, he or she is more likely to take it seriously and to consider it respectfully. Use of such forms indicates that you have done some careful observation, rather than impulsively decided that you or your child might have ADHD. You must clearly understand, however, that you are not the professional being consulted. The professional may gather other information that will change the picture. That is reasonably common. The burden is on the professional to clearly explain things if this happens.

Examples

Let us take the time to walk through two examples so that it is clear what contribution each section of this form makes.

JILL

On page 35 we see a form filled out for Jill, a 10-year-old fifth grader. Jill has a target behavior that is common with ADHD: not turning in assignments in class. Like all the symptoms of ADHD, however, this behavior is not exclusive to ADHD. We see that this behavior happens

Child Target Behavior Reporting Form

Jill
10 yrs. old
5th grade

1. What specific behavior is clearly seen?

   not turning in class assignments

2. How often does it happen?

   ☐ 1x/week   ☐ 1x/day   ☑ 2-5x/day

   ☐ 6-10x/day   ☐ 1x/hour   ☐ 2-5x/hour   ☐ more

3. How severe is this behavior?

   ☐ annoying   ☐ interrupts things

   ☐ disrupts everything around

   ☑ gets into trouble with rules

4. Where does this behavior occur?

   ☐ home   ☐ gym   ☑ classroom

   ☐ cafeteria   ☐ bus   ☐ individually

   ☐ car   ☐ stores   ☐ small group meetings

   ☐ hallways   ☐ offices   ☐ playground

   ☐ restaurants   ☐ businesses

   ☐ other _____

5. Who sees this behavior?

   ☑ mom   ☑ dad   ☑ teacher   ☐ coaches

   ☐ tutors   ☐ aides   ☑ counselors   ☑ principal

   ☐ specialists   ☐ neighbors   ☐ everyone

6. How long has this behavior existed?

   ☐ all life   ☐ 3 yrs on   ☐ 5 yrs on   ☐ just started

   ☑ specific years *started in 5th grade*

7. What have you tried to stop this behavior?

   grounding her, lecturing, buying an organizing notebook for her

8. What seems to work in reducing this behavior at least some of the time? *if you stand over her and make her do everything*

two to five times each day. In the interview we learn that this depends upon the number of assignments made for the day.

In Section 3 of the form, we learn that this target behavior is a severe problem. It is getting her in trouble with the rules. She is risking failure and possible retention. As might be assumed, this behavior occurs only in the classroom. It is noticed, however, by both parents, her teacher, a classroom aide, her guidance counselor, and her principal. There have been meetings with these staff members and the parents.

In Section 6 we learn a critical piece of information. This behavior only started in this current school year. After further inquiry, we learn that she did well in school during every previous school year. The parents reported three things they have tried to improve this target behavior: grounding her, lecturing her, and buying her an organizing notebook. Then, in the final section, we learn that they actually have tried four things. The fourth being standing over her and making her do her work item by item. Interestingly, none of the three things they remembered trying were reported as being helpful. They have found some success with standing over her and making her do everything.

The sensitive piece of information on this form is the fact that this target behavior has only started in the fifth grade. We have already discussed that ADHD is a lifelong neurobiological phenomenon. Therefore this notation will have to be understood more fully. More interviews with the family may reveal that she had been enrolled in a small, private school up through the fourth grade, and this private school had small classes with tolerant, flexible staff. This fifth-grade year may be her first experience in a large school, or it may be her first experience with moving from class to class every 40 minutes.

Another possible explanation might be that she has always attended the same school, but that her parents are going through a divorce this school year. Her difficulties with organization may be due to anxiety about what her parents might do, and what might happen to her world.

The reason that standing over her and making her do everything works for her is that it keeps at least one parent near her and makes her feel more secure.

There is also the real possibility that Jill's situation is a combination of all these things. She may have ADHD and her parents may be going through a divorce. There may also be stressors in school. Students may be picking on her. A teacher may be pushing too hard, or backing off and making too many excuses for her.

Using this form sharpens the focus of the inquiry. People can get to the critical questions faster by having so much of the essential information thoughtfully recorded in this way. Using this form does not eliminate further inquiry. It makes further inquiry much more productive.

DAN

Page 38 outlines the target behavior reporting form for Dan. Dan is a successful businessman who is irritating his family and friends, because he often does not hear important details in what they say to him. We see that this is reported to happen approximately once a day. It does not seem to be rated as too severe, but the rater indicated that it interrupts things. This behavior does not, apparently, occur in formal settings like the workplace, small group meetings, businesses, or offices. It is not noticed by business associates or neighbors. It is noticed by family members and friends.

This behavior is reported to have existed all his life. We see that Dan has tried some aggressive things to improve the problem, like taking a food supplement for a while and registering for a course in listening skills. These are not casual steps, and we get a hint at what may be driving these substantial efforts in the first item of Section 7: his wife gets mad at him.

It would be tempting to say that since this does not appear to affect his work or professional life, it is not all that important. There are

Adult Target Behavior Reporting Form

Dan 42 yrs. old

1. What specific behavior is clearly seen?

   misses important details of verbal information

2. How often does it happen?
   - ☐ 1x/week
   - ☑ 1x/day
   - ☐ 2-5x/day
   - ☐ 6-10x/day
   - ☐ 1x/hour
   - ☐ 2-5x/hour
   - ☐ more

3. How severe is this behavior?
   - ☐ annoying
   - ☑ interrupts things
   - ☐ disrupts everything around
   - ☐ gets into trouble with rules

4. Where does this behavior occur?
   - ☑ home
   - ☐ gym
   - ☐ classroom
   - ☐ cafeteria
   - ☐ bus
   - ☑ individually
   - ☑ car
   - ☑ stores
   - ☐ small group meetings
   - ☐ hallways
   - ☐ offices
   - ☐ playground
   - ☑ restaurants
   - ☐ businesses
   - ☐ other _____

5. Who sees this behavior?
   - ☑ spouse
   - ☐ mom
   - ☐ dad
   - ☑ siblings
   - ☑ relatives
   - ☐ supervisors
   - ☐ co-workers
   - ☐ specialists
   - ☑ children
   - ☐ neighbors
   - ☐ everyone

6. How long has this behavior existed?
   - ☑ all life
   - ☐ 3 yrs on
   - ☐ 5 yrs on
   - ☐ just started
   - ☐ specific years _____

7. What have you tried to stop this behavior?

   wife gets mad at him, he took a course in listening, bought food supplements to improve memory

8. What seems to work in reducing this behavior at least some of the time? *some friends tap him on the shoulder or use some introductory phrases before starting with the critical verbal information*

some red flags, however, that suggest that there may be something important to look into. This pattern is common with ADHD. The fact that the informant does not indicate that this is a problem in the workplace or formal settings may not be entirely accurate. Upon further interview that is more focused because of this information, we might learn that Dan has many little strategies for coping with this problem at work. He may have his secretary sit in on most meetings to pick up details he misses. He may have been passed up for many promotions for this problem, but still be valuable to the company at his present level. This seemingly tame item in Section 3, "interrupts things," may mean that career progress has been interrupted. Suddenly this may not be so tame.

It is also interesting that some of his friends have developed accommodations for him that appear to work. This suggests that they recognized a problem to the extent that they worked out some interventions for it. It does not appear that some of the most important people in his life, such as his wife and family, have picked up on these strategies yet. We should not dismiss the indicator on this form of the wife's expressed emotion lightly.

Again, the use of this form has accelerated the gathering of information and focused the direction of future inquiries in additional interviews.

Summary

The use of forms like these recognizes that individuals and families possess a lot of important information for the identifying process. Barkley [1997] has developed a set of forms for the same purpose (see Chapter 4). Families must appreciate their contribution to this process. They will be more likely to appreciate the importance of such forms if the process is valued by the professional they are working with.

When you maintain such forms and present the information to a professional, it is important to keep your anxiety level down. If the professional makes one comment, that does not mean that he or she will not consider another. Don't be afraid to put the most honest response down. Don't worry about what it might mean later. You may change responses, impressions, and conclusions. The value of this process is for you to find a starting point, to put a stake in the ground. Then you and your "team" can make additional measurements for further accuracy.

Chapter Six

· · · · · · · · · · · · · · · · · ·

Where to Go
for Help

NOW THAT YOU KNOW that attention-deficit/hyperactivity disorder (ADHD) is a neurobiological disorder, you know how different environments can have an impact upon it, and you have recorded relevant information, you can decide whether you believe that you are dealing with ADHD or not. If ADHD sounds like an appropriate diagnosis, where do you go for help?

Schools

If the person suspected of having ADHD is of school age (0-22), then a good starting point is with your school district. Federal laws have placed an increased burden of identification and programming on schools, which have access to school psychologists, administrators, school counselors, teachers, nurses, and aides who have experience with children. This experience usually gives them a knowledge of what normal behavior for the various age ranges is.

The typical preschool years (0-5) is an age range where some schools may have less experience. In some states, kindergarten was not mandatory until recently, but since the mid-1970s, federal education laws have mandated that schools be responsible for evaluations from birth through 22. Preschool programming is a fast-growing area in education. However, some schools are doing well with this age range, and some may just be getting into it.

You would be wise to ask questions. Call schools and ask administrators, ask staff members, ask secretaries. Ask for the phone numbers of parent organization officers and talk to them. As time goes on, you will increasingly discover that school staff usually have excellent experience and expertise in this area. (There are always the exceptions where a key staff member in the chain may be weak. It is something that you need to inform yourself about as an aggressive consumer of these services.)

Health Care Professionals

As Chapter 4 noted, health care professionals are generally involved in this process. Parents may wish to begin there, particularly with the younger children. The same kinds of questions should apply. Does this health care professional have sufficient experience with this age range, and with this suspected health concern? In most cases the answer will be yes, since this is such a common concern. As an assertive consumer, however, you need to determine the qualifications of any health care professional.

Community Resources

Schools and health professionals can direct you to other support groups in the community, to agencies that may exist for help, or to good sources for information. Many public libraries have books and videotapes on this subject that will give you much valuable information. Educational book stores or certain sections of general book stores also have books, tapes, and videotapes on this subject.

Some communities may have a school psychologist in private practice, pediatric neurologist, psychologist, or psychiatrist who has a wonderful reputation with just this disorder.

There are private schools that specialize in ADHD. There may be social workers or counselors of various kinds who have pursued special training and experience in this area. Depending upon your community, one of these may be the finest choice you could make.

Look in phone directories, call the local chamber of commerce, and ask the staff at schools and hospitals about whether they know of these options. The more you ask around, the better your chances of selecting an initial source for help that will be informed and competent.

Possibly the best source for help is a community support group. Some of these groups are well-organized. Some have regular meetings, publications, and conferences that are local, statewide, national, and international. The process of learning who might be the best professional to consult is greatly facilitated by a community support group. If the support group has been around for any length of time, members will have a wealth of information about the various providers in your community.

Most of these organizations are informal in nature. They provide a setting where people with common experiences can meet, share strategies, and share solutions. If the group has been in existence for some time, it is common to have members of all ages. Veteran members can help new members get through the various systems they will encounter, since they usually know about the irregularities in the systems and how to cope with them.

For example, there are many individual responses to these disorders. Sometimes a medication will appear to work well for a number of years and then, mysteriously, appear to no longer work at all. These support groups often have families that have lived through these variations and can reassure the new member about what is going on and what it does and does not mean. (I have been asked to speak, periodically, at some of their meetings and I am often impressed with what members have to teach me.)

There are camp experiences for children with ADHD as well. Respite for the primary caregivers is often a need that is overlooked. If there are organized outings or camp experiences, this might be an opportunity for the parents to also get some relief and regroup their composure and strength.

Some parenting classes are designed to give parents the tools for handling children with ADHD. There are specific skills that can be learned for dealing with the challenges of this disorder at home, while visiting others, in the car or in some other transportation, and in public places like a restaurant, store, or mall.

This instruction is available individually in a private office, but it is often available in such settings as support groups or parenting classes. Ideally, your health care provider or local public school should know about these services, but you may have to do some searching yourself. Those that offer these services are not really trying to keep them confidential. They frequently hear that people never knew they existed and that they wished they had found the services years earlier.

Considerations for Adults with ADHD

For those beyond the public school years, all the advice above is true, except that pertaining to schools. Your family doctor or a local mental health professional specializing in educational or learning concerns will probably be the two most likely starting points. It remains important to inquire about the level of experience these people have with adult ADHD. The experience varies dramatically in the community. While the information in this book will arm you in helping them gain necessary experience, it is easier on you if they already have such experience.

This search does not end your responsibility in being an informed consumer, but it does help to reduce the possibility of an initial mistake.

CHAPTER SEVEN

. . . .

Intervention: Medical

THERE ARE ONLY TWO broad classes of interventions that reliably offer help: medical and psychosocial. (Psychosocial relates to the environment and relationships of the individual.) Enthusiastic proponents have reported and recommended many other interventions. My concern is that these interventions lack the robust research support needed to endorse a reliable intervention tool across populations. It is unwise, and unnecessary, to argue with individuals who feel that other interventions have been a big help for them. There appear to be individual responses to other courses of action.

For our purposes, however, we will stick with recommendations that have been shown to be helpful to a large percentage of people trying them. It is not wise to think of medication or psychosocial interventions as an either/or decision. Those dealing with attention-deficit/hyperactivity disorder (ADHD) might generally elect to use both together. This would be the best practice. There are many, however, who elect to use only one or the other. In the case of psychosocial intervention, discussed in Chapter 8, this single approach might be driven by concerns about taking medications. In the case of medication, this single approach might be driven by problems with the schedule and the demands of psychosocial interventions alone.

McMurray [1995] found that 75-80% of people properly identified with ADHD show a positive response to the use of medication in the reduction of the ADHD symptoms that interfere with their success. Barkley elaborates:

> We must keep in mind that 70-75 percent of children generically diagnosed as ADHD without regard to comorbidity respond well to stimulant medication. Also, we know that up to 92 percent of those well-diagnosed as ADHD, where ADD without hyperactivity or comorbid anxiety disorders are removed from consideration, respond well to medication. Hence, it will be a formidable task, indeed, to find an instrument, Neurometrics or otherwise, that could exceed this type of predictive accuracy of drug response based on sound clinical diagnosis alone. [1994, p. 3]

This is so encouraging that to pursue other interventions and ignore medication is to bypass a powerful tool. There may be good reasons to bypass this approach, but these decisions should be made with this knowledge in mind. There are always concerns about medication. Few people want to take medications. Even fewer want to administer them to their children. But many people are utilizing medications, and the willingness to do so is increasing [Connor et al. 1996]. A close look at the decision process that they use before electing this path would be helpful here.

Before anyone should consider taking a medication for ADHD, he or she should not only get a comprehensive assessment, but also an impression of how severe the symptoms are. ADHD is a "spectrum" disorder, meaning that there can be milder cases and more severe cases. With milder cases, people may initially prefer to handle the symptoms with changes in school and home rules, with prompts, and the other strategies that will be discussed in Chapter 12.

Some time ago, the American Academy of Pediatrics [1987] issued a statement that medication should be administered only after professionals and caregivers have attempted a number of environmental interventions. I hope that this process of exhausting environmental interventions both at home and at school would be part of the identification process leading up to a thorough diagnosis. In most cases it is, but there are many stories of caregivers who rush to a medical intervention on the slightest presentation of symptoms.

In more severe cases, utilizing medications seems to be an easier decision. The most compelling argument for this goes something like this. The major concern with utilizing medications is the fear of side effects. Even if medications have been shown to have few, there is a residual fear in most of us that there may be some that will only show up much later. But, going through 12 years of school being inattentive, hyperactive, and in trouble almost constantly with adults and peers, also has severe side effects. When caregivers look at the extreme social problems that have developed, and their impact upon the individual's ability to get the maximum benefit out of school, the decision gets easier [Richter-Sand 1995; Brooks 1994]. While there are stories about parents who rush to medications for the slightest symptoms, this does not account for the majority of the use of medications for this purpose.

There are a range of medications used. One class is stimulants. Another is mild antidepressants. Some are medications typically used for other disorders that have been found to have positive effects upon ADHD symptoms. Some health care professionals begin with the stimulants. Some begin with one of the milder antidepressants based upon their clinical experience in their area. Clearly these are medical decisions made, hopefully, by people who are well-informed and who struggle to follow the most responsible path in the care of their patients. This appears to follow a trial-and-error approach, with the guiding rule being the lowest levels of medication that achieve the desired effects.

One complicating issue that makes this process difficult in some cases is the problem of comorbid disorders. (Comorbid disorders exist together and one disorder plays a major part in the symptom development of the others.) This has an influence upon the selection of medications.

Consumers of these services can take some comfort in the fact that the medical approach to ADHD is under intense and constant scrutiny from governmental agencies and private interest groups. Because the incidence rate is so high for ADHD (5% of the general population is the widely accepted figure), there are accusations that this disorder is overidentified and that the medications for it are overutilized. While this frequently generates sensational media coverage that may frighten some people, it also drives a lot of research. As this research comes in, the general trend is encouraging.

Methylphenidate (Ritalin) is the medication that is perhaps most commonly associated with ADHD. It appears to be getting safer and safer as more studies come in. Side effects that we used to caution parents about a few years ago appear to be unconfirmed in the newer research. For example, there used to be speculation that the use of stimulants tended to stunt growth slightly—around 2%—in some individuals. With additional study [Spencer et al. 1996], this now does not appear to be the case. It seems that for periods of time growth may slow slightly, but this is naturally corrected at other periods in the person's lifespan.

Another early concern that appears to be explained by more research is the concern about some medications causing Tourette's syndrome. There was a lot of anxiety about the use of some medications possibly pushing someone into symptoms associated with Tourette's syndrome. In subsequent research it appears that this is not a well-founded concern. What appears to have happened is that individuals who were showing early signs of Tourette's syndrome were aggressively picked up for treatment for ADHD due to the symptoms commonly found in both disorders. The fact that they were on their way to Tourette's syndrome was apparently coincidental, rather than the treatment for ADHD being causal. Gadow and others [1995] reported that methylphenidate appears to be safe even with children with comorbid tic disorders. Finally, recent research has dispelled some concerns that methylphenidate administered in the late afternoon might cause insomnia [Kent et al. 1995].

On the negative side, Barkley [1997a] recently included an "Editor's Alert" in a publication noting that the makers of Cylert (pemoline) had modified their labeling and recommendations as a result of a review of postmarketing experience showing a small number of cases of liver failure in adults and children. The recommendation suggested "that Cylert should not ordinarily be considered as a first-line drug therapy for attention deficit hyperactivity disorder (ADHD)" [Barkley 1997a, p. 16]. Interestingly, some are deciding to switch to another medication. Some are staying with Cylert, believing the incidence rate to be negligible. And some who initially decided to switch to another medication have returned to that medication because it worked so well for them.

Adderall (mixed salts of single amphetamine) may be the "new kid on the block." It had been around under a different name, but in 1994 it was purchased by another pharmaceutical company and now goes by this name. Swanson and others report a double-blind, placebo-controlled crossover study that recommends that Adderall "be added to the list of stimulants to be tried in a comprehensive evaluation of this class of medications" [Swanson et al. 1998a, p. 525]. This recommendation is predicated on the belief that additional dose-response studies examining more complete dosing regimen comparisons will confirm the relative efficacy of Adderall in treating different populations of ADHD patients.

There are ongoing studies about the relationship between ADHD and substance use disorders [Wilens et al 1997; Biederman et al. 1997]; substance abuse [Horner & Scheibe 1997]; cigarette smoking [Milberger et al. 1997]; antisocial and drug abuse disorders [Mannuzza et al. 1993]; negative academic outcomes or antisocial acts [Barkley et al. 1990]; and educational achievement and occupational rank in adulthood [Slomkowski et al. 1995]. It has been suggested that in some cases smoking may even be an effort at self-medication [Conners 1996]. It is important to note that these high-risk behaviors appear to occur with ADHD. Since people have no choice about having ADHD, the risks must be accepted and treated intelligently. If families can reduce the stressors and the trauma a child lives with through medical and psychosocial interventions, that will certainly make today more pleasant even if it does little to alter long-range predictions. This was most eloquently clarified by Goldstein [1997]:

> Not a single study has been published suggesting that if children take Ritalin, they will turn out to be better adults. Yet there are well over 500 studies suggesting that if they take their Ritalin today, there is a reduced likelihood their mothers and teachers will respond to them in angry, frustrated ways. Although we choose to believe that if each day of a life is better, future life outcome will be better, we have yet to demonstrate this in populations of children with ADHD. Thus, families must be helped to understand that treatments for ADHD are directed at relieving symptoms. However, factors powerful in predicting good life outcomes for all children are critically important for children at risk, such as those with ADHD. Such factors include strong family attachments, developing appropriate social relations, and locating activities in life to experience success and develop a sense of efficacy. [1997, p. 5]

I list these matters to illustrate two things. First, people have individual responses and opinions to medication itself. Second, both government regulators and consumer researchers have focused a great deal of scrutiny upon these medications. I believe that we are justified with having a reasonable level of comfort with the supervised use of medications. Nevertheless, no one would suggest that further research is unnecessary.

Similarly, no one would suggest that anyone—no matter what the research says—will not have a unique, individual response to treatment. This is why choosing to follow a medication intervention is a matter between an individual and his or her primary health care provider. I am chagrined by reports I occasionally hear that individuals in related professions will direct parents or individuals to ask for specific medications and make claims that the instruments they use or their own experience enables them to predict exact dosage levels. There is evidence [Rapport & Denney 1997] that even body weight—historically considered a good predictor of dosage levels—is not a good predictor of clinical response.

Greater precision in predicting treatment dosage may well be possible in the future as continued progress is made in research; however, I know of no information currently available that is replicated sufficiently to make such practice helpful. For now, it remains a matter of medical judgment, trials, and observation.

CHAPTER EIGHT

· · · · · · · · · · · · · · · · · ·

Intervention: Psychosocial

PSYCHOSOCIAL INTERVENTION is behavior modification, and behavior modification revolves around one rule: Any behavior that exists, exists because it is being rewarded. Sometimes the link between the behavior and the reward is obvious, sometimes it is quite subtle. Usually, people agree about what is rewarding and what is punishing, but sometimes an individual's perception of what is rewarding or punishing is unique and unpredictable. Behavior modification is tinkering with the rewards and punishments in his or her environment to change the person's behavior. Conceptually, it is really that simple. The two major challenges of behavior modification are identifying what the person finds to be rewarding or punishing, and then providing those rewards or punishments in an appropriate, therapeutic manner.

Sometimes the rewards are material (candy, tokens, or money); sometimes they are social (praise, hugs, recognition, love). Some rewards are more powerful than others. Some rewards start out powerful but fade in potency over time. Understanding these matters is helpful in using this powerful intervention for attention-deficit/hyperactivity disorder (ADHD).

Behavior Modification Is for Everyone

Some parents sit in an office and listen politely to instructions about behavior modification and go home with no intention of doing it, because they think it is only something specialists drag out for people with problems. They fear that putting these recommendations in place will make them look "special" and different. While they are not oppositional people and would never tell a specialist that they are not going to do it, they resist. So the first thing that should be covered is that behavior modification is natural. It happens naturally in all homes in some fashion or another.

I could argue that governmental legislatures are nothing but behavior modification factories. If you locate your business in this city you will receive a tax credit (reward). If you dump pollution into a river you will receive a fine (punishment). The government has found that most people comply with the behavior modification plans they have created, but some do not. For those that do not, the government has to create further rules.

The best example of this is speeding in traffic. Shortly after cars were introduced, the safety hazard of speeding cars arose. The government instituted speed limits, posted speed limits, and made provisions for fines to be levied against an offender. (The amount of the first fines would be laughable today!) Legislatures found that they had to increase the fine for this behavior modification to continue to be effective.

Personally, I find the current fine structure quite punishing and I am motivated to avoid getting a ticket. I have a few friends, however, who are doing far better financially and consider the amounts of today's fines to be small change. So legislatures found that they need to go back and tinker with the plan still more. They came up with another layer of punishment called points. If a person gets so many points in a given period of time, he can have his license revoked. The plan's fine tuning appears to have effectively reigned in these wealthy friends.

We should see that setting up these reward and punishment plans, or behavior modification plans, is natural. It goes on every day. And because the people we work with constantly change, the plan needs to be modified from time to time as well. It is an unrealistic expectation to think anyone can set up a behavior modification plan once and it will work well for a long time. Year after year legislatures tinker with the rules to ensure that they are working. They have had to create layers of consequences when some people defy some of the rules.

Whether parents like the term behavior modification or not, they are practicing it now, they have all their lives, and they cannot escape it. The question is, are they practicing it in the most successful way they can? Or are they making some common errors that derail their best hopes?

Most parents sitting in my office when we talk about behavior modification will say, "Oh, I've tried that. It doesn't work." They are telling the truth. Most parents have stumbled across some good plans in their efforts to handle matters themselves. So why did these plans not work? There are three reasons that behavior modification plans *appear* not to work. Please notice the word "appear." There is no serious debate anymore that behavior modification does not work. But it can *appear* not to work if 1) the consequences used are not potent, 2) the consequences fade in potency over time, or 3) the person being treated with this plan decides to "call the bluff" of the person carrying out the plan.

Potent Consequences

If you tell a young child that when he gets his homework done he will be allowed to watch the evening news program, you may not see the child modify his behavior. While this example sounds ridiculous, it is amazing how out of touch some parents are about what a child would consider a meaningful reward or punishment. You do not have a plan at all if your plan fails to account for the child's perception of the consequences.

Potency in children is determined by what they like, what is cool, and how close the consequence is in time to the present. A child may be more motivated by a cheap fruit-flavored candy than she or he would be by an expensive piece of real fruit. Children may be more motivated by the chance to stay up a half hour later than by going to an expensive art museum or a concert.

It is important to notice that there are many rewards that are quite potent that do not cost much or anything. Stop for a moment and think about your own childhood. What were some of the most rewarding moments you had with family? I suspect that they would revolve around when a parent genuinely listened to you, or when a parent read a book with you, or played a game with you, or took you somewhere and let you select what you wanted to do. Some of these cost you some of your time, but if you have been busy and absent from your child, this attention may represent some of the most potent rewards for your planning.

Time spent making lists of what the child finds most rewarding and most punishing is time well-spent, because your plan must take into account the child's perception of these things, not your own.

Consequences Fade in Potency

A parent may have put together a perfect behavior modification plan that worked for a while but mysteriously stopped working within a week or two. Sometimes, consequences that are potent initially will fade in potency over time. If you offer a young child some money for a certain behavior, you may see a nice increase in that behavior for a while. After that child piles up a little surplus of money, however, he may believe that he has all he will ever need and the use of money will fade as a potent reward.

This is not different for adults. A company may offer employees financial incentives for working overtime. Most employees will jump at that for a while; however, at some point they will decide that some free time at home with their families is more rewarding than any additional money. Employers will find that there is a limit to how rewarding money is.

The same is true for punishments. If you told a student that if he failed to hand in his work he would lose TV privileges, this might be upsetting initially. Sometimes, however, students will decide that losing TV is less punishing than doing certain kinds of homework. So a plan that initially got the student's attention effectively broke down over time.

This also happens when the consequence is delayed too long. If you tell a child that if she behaves a certain way for the entire school year, she will get to go to a major amusement park the following summer, that will be exciting at first. The reward is probably too far off, however, to retain that excitement day after day. The same is true for punishments. If you told that same child that if she engaged in a certain unwanted behavior any more for the entire school year, she will not get to go to the amusement park when the rest of the family goes. Again, she will want to meet that goal, but the more immediate day-to-day rewards of misbehaving seem to outweigh those placed so far off on the horizon.

For this reason, parents learn that they have to change the menu of consequences. Therefore, they need to have a large list of consequences to work from.

Calling Your Bluff

Perhaps the most difficult reason behavior modification plans appear not to work is that some children call your bluff. It always amazes parents when they think about how clever their children are at manipulating them. Many children know just how long a parent will continue with a plan when it appears to not be working. If the child does not like the plan, he may decide to hold out, refuse to change his behavior, or even get a little worse, and he knows when his parents will abandon the plan and go back to business as usual. Children have this kind of knowledge, because for many years they only had to specialize in two people, their parents. That was their whole world. Parents had their attentions divided with learning the rules of banks, insurance companies, employers, social clubs, religious organizations, political organizations, salesmen, sports clubs, etc. Their children have focused only on them. They have done their homework, and they know how to wiggle around and get what they want at least some of the time.

So when parents have crafted an effective plan, they need to commit to outlast this possible trap to the plan's working. This process is quite common. It is not evil. The child will use the same skills for getting ahead in the work world. They are good skills to have. It is just that parents need to understand that the child has these skills and is willing to use them on his parents.

Establish a Relationship

Capitalizing on the intangible rewards, few rewards are as powerful as a positive interpersonal relationship. Students with ADHD often live with a lot of criticism. Their behaviors draw negative attention from caregivers. It does not take long for this to depress a child. A steady stream of harsh treatment will erode any mental health. This ultimately makes the child uncomfortable, sensitive, and more inclined to act in maladaptive ways. This, of course, circles around and elicits more criticism from caregivers.

One of the first things to get thrown out of any relationship between a caregiver and a child with an ADHD is positive, pleasant, quality interactions. It seems like most of the caregiver's time is spent in correction, and when that is not immediately required, the caregiver seeks ways to get away from the child for respite. Therefore the only interaction the child has with most caregivers is negative.

One of the first lines of attack, therefore, is to engage in activities that will build up a relationship. In Russell Barkley's parenting program [1997c] for oppositional and noncompliant children, he calls his opening activity for parents, "Paying Attention to Your Child's Good Play Behavior."

Barkeley's idea is to get parents to remember the feelings they had when a supervisor at work made demands, but seemed to pay no attention to them otherwise. Bad supervisors do not listen to their subordinates, and do not take time to know what the subordinate is doing. Barkley suggests that children may have these feelings about parents in highly stressful homes. In Barkley's plan, the child is allowed to pick the activity.

Suppose the child picks playing catch with a baseball in the backyard. The parent is encouraged to make frequent comments about how the child is doing the activity. Examples might be, "Wow, you really dove for that one!" or, "Nice stop!" or "You really burned that one in for a strike!"

This is a powerful technique, because it introduces the child to something that has likely been missing for a long time in many cases: quality, pleasant, adult responses to him. Or as Barkley puts it: "This is often contrary to the parents' current practice of ignoring positive child behaviors while attending or responding only to the disruptive or negative ones" [Barkley 1997c, p. 105].

Paying attention to a child builds a sense of relationship. It makes the child feel some care for the adult and, therefore, improves the child's motivation to inhibit some behaviors, and to cooperate with the adult's agenda.

For tutors, therapists, or small group teachers, this might be partially accomplished by leaving the classroom or office for the first session or two and walking to a neighborhood store for some candy or ice cream. This warmer and more personal atmosphere may help build a sense of relationship between you and the child that will make all future work easier and more successful. Take this time to find out about the child. Learn more about his personality, his likes, and dislikes, his hobbies, and interests.

Do not rush too quickly into your agenda or program. Attend to the child's needs for comfort, trust, and appreciation. The child, after all, has to size you up as much as you have to size him up.

Planned Ignoring

Have you ever noticed that some people have fewer management problems with an ADHD child than others? This is because some people are good at ignoring irritants that do not threaten to cause bigger problems. Others create unnecessary tension in a situation by being fussy about many things that do not really matter. Let me illustrate.

I had been saying no to one of my sons a number of times one Saturday morning. He was about 7 at the time. It seemed like he was going from one thing to another and each thing was violating some household rule that I thought needed to be discouraged. Then he started playing with a door knob on a clothes closet in the hallway. He turned the knob and let it snap back. Then he turned the knob the other way and let it snap back again. Back and forth, this went on for a few seconds. I found the sound irritating and was just about to bark at him and tell him to quit it. Then I thought, I have been saying no to him quite a bit lately. Is this behavior really hurting anything? I realized that these knobs were designed to do this for years without wearing out. I decided that the matter needed no correction at all. I ignored it. Within about 10 seconds, he got tired of it and stopped.

There are a huge number of these behaviors that a child with ADHD does, which irritate his parents. One parent criticized a child for having his cap set too tight in the back. She thought it would make red marks on the child's forehead. A parent might be irritated by a child's swinging his feet, or hitting them together while they are sitting and talking. There are long lists of these kinds of irritants.

Ask yourself: Is the child going to hurt himself or others? Does this activity interfere with the child's ability to pay attention to what is being said or done? Is the child likely to give up the activity soon if you just ignore it? You would be amazed at how many parents are fighting these unnecessary battles and at how tensions are rising with each one. Most of them could be successfully ignored.

Give the Child Some Influence

There are many situations where a child may wish to exert his influence in the program. He may decide that some small accommodation to the plan is necessary for that day. It is your job to determine how important your agenda is, and whether it will be adversely affected by the child's modification. If it does not matter, allow the child to have that influence in the procedures for that day. The child appreciates having his influence accepted in the plan. That appreciation may well express itself in slightly more cooperation with the parent's larger program for that day.

Make a Fuss When He Is Compliant

In the worst case of ADHD that I ever saw, the child was compliant with the parents' demands or expectations 75% of the time. We often fail to recognize the overwhelming majority of the time when the child is complying with expectations.

The child is usually sitting in my office with his parents while they are explaining many of the problems they are having with him. Generally, the child sits there reasonably quietly, even though the conversation is about all his failings. That is a situation that would make most of us squirm. Often I have to point out to the parents how compliant he has been in this setting. There is almost an expression of surprise when I mention this. Parents need to recognize compliance and make a big fuss. They would experience more success if they commented upon the thing that they want when they see it, namely that he is being cooperative, and that he is making the discussion go smoothly. (Thanks to the television program "Sesame Street," most children know what the word "cooperate" means.)

The research has been telling us for years that you will likely see more of any behavior you reward. Let me illustrate again. A 7-year-old girl was walking around a large block with her parents. Another couple was walking toward them and her father asked what their names were so that he could speak to them using their name. The girl said, "Those are the Millers." When the family got closer to the Millers, the father said hello to them, calling their name. The Millers returned the greeting, calling the family by their name.

After the family proceeded beyond hearing, the father turned to his daughter and said, "Wow, you have a great memory for names." For the rest of the way around the block, she pointed out that the Smiths lived there, and the Browns lived there, and so forth. Without asking, the father received much more of the behavior that he encouraged in his daughter.

This is such a powerful secret that I'm sure many readers will have made the following experience. Have you ever noticed that if someone tells a joke that is effective (it makes people in the group laugh in a big way), then that person will tell the exact same joke a second time immediately after? It is almost like a gravitational pull. Even though she knows that it will not be funny the second time, the quest for the encouragement of being so successful with a joke will cause her to try it again in spite of what is known.

The idea is to take advantage of this powerful feature of human nature. If your child shows some compliance to rules or expectations, make a big fuss. The thrill of making an important adult in their lives so happy, or so impressed, will almost inevitably make them do more of the same.

CHAPTER NINE

· ·

Basic Steps in Behavior Modification

PARENTS LOOK FOR specific instruction and guidance from books or experts, only to find that when they take the instructions home, the instructions do not work for them. It would be better if parents took a little more time to absorb the core concepts of behavior modification and become experts themselves. Then they can craft their own plans and modify them as needed over time. Rather than look for books that spell out the steps with greater and greater elaboration, learn how to create your own steps, beginning with these basic ones:

- Identify the target behaviors

- List rewards and punishments

- Draft the contract

- Carry out the contract

- Evaluate the contract

- Modify the contract

Identify the Target Behaviors

Identify the top few most disturbing behaviors the child does. Be sure to list them as observable behaviors that everyone would agree upon when seen. "Poking her sister with sharp objects" is better than "being mean," and "not completing the second half of homework assignments" is preferable to "never follows through with things."

Target behaviors must be seen. They must be "countable" by anyone, not just the parent. This is the only way you can be sure that you are making progress with your plan. You can wish that the child was "feeling better about herself," or "takes more interest in school work," but if other observers cannot count up what you are talking about, you cannot get a clear measure of progress or regression.

Write a list of behaviors at the top of a piece of paper. You may create a longer list at first, but you will want to reduce the list to one or two behaviors for getting started.

List Rewards and Punishments

Have those who know the individual best make a list of the 10 things he likes the most and the 10 things he dislikes the most. After everyone has made his or her list separately, compare the lists. Certainly there will be much overlap, but this is how you can generate a menu of rewards and punishments fairly quickly. You will have a list of items to try. Some will work, some will not.

As you work with this plan, you may add items to each list. Over time, the list will naturally change as well. If the people making this list know the individual, this list will be valuable. It will contain potent rewards and punishments. Have confidence in that.

Draft the Contract

Two rules help these contracts. First, keep them simple. Second, involve the individual in the drafting of the contract. The contract can be a fairly simple statement along the lines of "If ... then." For example: "If you go one whole day turning in every assignment given to you at school, then you will be allowed to stay up one-half hour later that evening." "If you go one full day without hitting your sister, then you will be able to eat your favorite breakfast cereal the following morning." "If you go one full day responding to verbal commands with one or fewer reminders, then you will be allowed to run the TV's remote control from 7:00 to 8:00 P.M. that evening."

Notice that these statements all involve a reward to follow quickly on the heels of doing the desired (positive) behavior for a short period of time. The time duration is short. The reward is immediate, and it is something the individual highly desires.

These contracts can also involve the punishment of undesired behaviors. For example: "If you hit your sister, then you will have to go to bed one-half hour earlier that evening." "For every missing assignment, you will lose 30 minutes of TV time that evening." "For every time you fail to do a verbal request, after the first reminder you will have to sit in a time-out chair for 15 minutes and then go back and still do the initial request."

It is widely agreed that positive rewards tend to have more potency in changing behavior. This is not just because it is popular to be positive. Many parents have found that their children can become almost immune to punishments. Many people find that punishments do not work all that well. It is just human nature to think of them first.

I like to think of the rewards as the carrot that you dangle out in front of the mule, and punishments as the "stick" that you threaten the mule with. I see no reason why there should not be both a carrot and stick in every plan. The contract can contain both a reward for the desired behavior and a punishment for the presence of the undesired behavior. This idea of having a range of positive and negative strategies is clearly summarized by Edwards [1995], who suggests that for "minor" misbehavior, you could use ignoring or praise. What he calls "mid-level" might include penalties like, "If you make your bed, you can watch TV before school; if you don't make your bed, no TV." He suggests that time-out be reserved for major behavioral problems that did not respond to earlier levels.

There can also be levels of both rewards and punishments. For example, in addition to having a reward for doing the desired behavior at the end of every day, you could also offer a reward if the child goes five consecutive days receiving the first reward. Five consecutive days receiving this first level of reward could also trigger an additional, bigger reward. Similarly, for each specific time the student does the desired behavior within the day, he could receive a more concrete reward like a piece of candy, a pat on the back, a hug, or an encouraging word.

The age of the individual in question plays an important part in this planning. Older people can wait longer for a bigger reward over a longer period of time. Young people generally need to see immediate rewards to sustain their effort and interest.

One unexpected benefit from walking through these steps this deliberately is that it forces parents and children to communicate more specifically about what they want. The step of writing down what the target behavior is, for example, may be the first time the child has actually heard that specific request. Often the parent expresses a list of vague complaints that greatly upset them, but they are not especially clear about what they want. If this is the case, these plans often work quickly. Children reason that if this is what their parents want, no problem, and the behavior changes rapidly.

I have repeatedly found that just the process of having parents spell out their goals in specific, measurable terms has actually helped the child figure out what exactly is making a parent so upset.

Carry Out the Contract

Once the contract is written, put it into place. It will be helpful to keep a simple log so that you can know—or measure—how often things have happened. This will be valuable for the step where you modify the contract. It is important to put the contract into place and leave it in place for a while to ensure that you have given the plan a chance to work. It is this decision of sticking with the contract for long enough that is so important. Millions of excellent plans have been abandoned by parents too quickly and, therefore, have never been given the chance to prove themselves. It is this point that enables many parents to say those most dreaded words to a therapist: "Oh, I've tried that. It doesn't work."

Evaluate the Contract

Decide upon a specific date when you will meet and discuss how this plan worked. If it worked fine, you may wish to extend it. You may wish to modify it, or you may decide that it is no longer necessary. The fact that you have an established date when you will examine the plan tends to increase the plan's power. It provides a level of supervision that will tend to make people take the plan more seriously.

On page 68 is a model form that a family may wish to adapt to meet their needs. If the child is too young to read, perhaps you can attach pictures that will prompt the child's memory about the key elements of the plan.

THINGS GET WORSE BEFORE THEY GET BETTER

Allow me to relate a favorite story of my intern supervisor, Stewart Keller. (I am not aware that this has been published anywhere, but if it has, I'd be delighted to give credit in a following printing.) This insight is absolutely critical to increasing the chances of the success of these plans.

If you put the correct change in a soft drink vending machine and push a button for a selection and nothing comes out, what do you do? Most people say that they hit the machine. Some jiggle the coin return. Some kick the machine. Most get upset. When asked whether they would put more money in the machine if they were thirsty, and

Behavior Modification Plan

Target behavior:

The plan:

Contracted reward:

Contracted punishment:

Evaluate the contract:

Signatures:

there were no other machine or drinking fountain around, most say that they would. They might assume that the machine failed to count correctly and they would try again. If the machine continued to give nothing in return, essentially everyone asked agreed that they would not continue putting more money in the machine.

What has happened in this familiar experience is that the person approaching the soft drink machine does so expecting an old, familiar rule. The rule is that so much money gets one can of a soft drink. In this situation, however, the machine has changed the rule. The new rule is that any amount of money gets nothing from the machine. When people first encounter the change in the rule, they get violent. They get worse and demand that the old rule apply. They even try to force the old rule by putting in more money. If the machine sticks to the new rule, people quickly learn the new rule and modify their behavior in accordance with the new rule. They stop demanding the old rule by putting more money in the machine.

Then why are people surprised when they go home from a behavior specialist's office armed with a new approach to handling their child's misbehavior and find that their child gets worse when first encountering the new rule? It is because the behavior specialist has failed to warn them of this common feature of human nature. Because of this, more plans have been thrown out the window that were perfectly fine and would have worked. Not only do parents give up on that plan, but they lose faith in behavior modification generally. Any future office they consult will hear those dreaded words, "Oh, I've tried that; it doesn't work," when they bring up behavior management strategies.

The parents are being absolutely truthful. They have tried it. It did not work in the time they allowed for it to work. It is extremely likely that the only flaw in the design was how long they gave the plan to work. It is not surprising that parents did not give it long to work if they saw their child's behavior getting worse as a result of the introduction of the plan. Without being warned of this almost certain course in most children, it is exactly what a good parent should do.

To look at this graphically, consider Figure 1, on page 71. The horizontal axis is the passing of time. The vertical axis is behavior getting worse.

Parents are concerned that their child is throwing temper tantrums three times a day. They live with this concern for four weeks before they talk to a behavior specialist about it. The behavior specialist gives them a plan to take home that will reward the child for not throwing temper tantrums and punish the child for throwing them. On that fourth week (marked by the left side of the shaded box), the parents faithfully put the plan into effect.

Just as the soft drink machine story would predict, this child gets worse immediately upon encountering this change in the rule. We can see that for a little more than one week this child actually has more temper tantrums on average every day. The parents have been armed with this expectation and stick to the new rule through thick or thin. Then, mysteriously, somewhere between the fifth and sixth week, the behavior starts to decline in frequency. From the sixth week on, the behavior slowly but steadily continues to drop until it reaches ranges that are typical of all other children the same age as this child.

These parents, so armed with the proper information, will have a positive experience with this contract, even though they had to endure some increase in misbehavior for nearly two weeks. They will value behavior modification and will understand how and why it works.

The big question is: how wide does that shaded box have to be? How long does a parent have to put up with this increase in misbehavior before the plan begins working and reduces misbehavior? That depends upon a lot: how potent the rewards or punishments are, how well designed the plan is, and how consistent the parent has been in the past. If the parent has never tried a behavior modification contract

Figure 1. Behavior Over Time

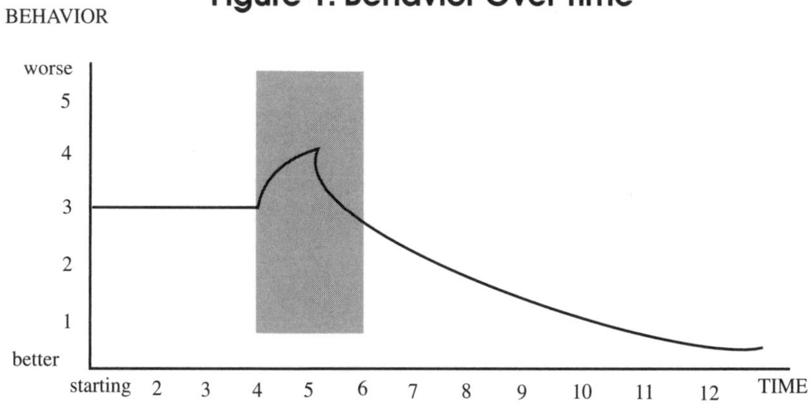

BEHAVIOR

and has, therefore, never changed the rules and then reversed himself, it is likely that this shaded box will not be too wide. If, on the other hand, the parent has made many changes in the home rules only to have the child rebel and misbehave to get those rules thrown out over and over, that shaded box may be rather long. That parent has unintentionally trained the child that, if the child does not like a rule, all he has to do is misbehave enough and the rule will be abandoned. This is a common development in many homes.

Modify the Contract

Even the best plans will fade in potency over time. It is necessary to tinker with the contract from time to time to ensure that rewards and punishments are still potent, and that time lines and outcomes are appropriate. This is different than giving up on the plan if it does not work. This is taking a plan that did work somewhat, or would work, and finetuning it to ensure that it continues to work.

I said that legislatures are huge behavior modification experts. An example of this finetuning can come from them. The legislature is constantly tinkering with tax laws to modify people's behavior. They call this "social engineering," and it makes a big impact on economies and business trends. So over the course of a behavior modification plan, finetuning needs to be done for the plans to remain potent in their goal of modifying an individual's behavior.

If you are having trouble knowing when it is appropriate to modify this behavioral contract, and when you are giving in to a child's ploy to get the contract abandoned, an objective behavior specialist can help you. Often, parents are too close emotionally to be able to see these issues objectively.

CHAPTER TEN

· · · · · · · · · · · · · ·

Measuring Behavior

ONCE ATTENTION-DEFICIT/HYPERACTIVITY disorder (ADHD) is correctly identified, it is not usually a matter of sending the family out with a single intervention strategy that will be robust and effective without follow-up. Interventions need to be explored, adjusted, modified, or abandoned, depending upon the individual's response to them.

When you are modifying human behavior, you are trying to harness something natural. Like canoeing down a river, you need to stick a paddle in every now and then to adjust the direction you are going. You would not think of aiming a canoe in a certain direction at the top of a run and expecting never to make a course adjustment along the way. The same is true for coping with the symptoms of ADHD. It is true for the family and it is true for the professionals involved.

With any intervention, you should take care to measure progress objectively. Interventions can be expensive or hard work. To justify continuing the commitment, there must be genuine improvement and not just wishful thinking. It can be difficult to measure. People who have lived with symptoms all their lives may have trouble identifying clearly what they are and whether they have changed.

With many disorders, we know that people can reduce or eliminate their symptoms for a short time. Therefore, while they are complying with treatment recommendations, they may be so eager for the treatment to work that they influence its success for a while. An accurate measurement of a treatment's success must cover a longer period of time.

Another problem with measuring treatment success is that people can have major blind spots about their own symptoms. Some people never see their own faults. Others can only see their faults. For these reasons, you need to find objective methods for the measurement of success. Ideally, you need objective observers other than the individual, or his family, to improve the accuracy of measurement.

The inconsistent presentation of ADHD symptoms also challenges professionals to monitor treatment strategies effectively. Professionals must work with the children and their families to establish target behavioral goals and then to objectively evaluate those goals frequently to ensure that improvement in behavior is really being seen. This chapter presents some strategies for measuring behavior.

Identify Target Behaviors

It is not helpful to begin a treatment and just hope that some of the problem behaviors are improved. It is better to identify several target behaviors that you want to see improved. This will not only make one's evaluation of the progress more focused, it will help you check to be sure that your target behaviors are reasonable in the first place. Write down two or three behaviors that you wish your treatment plan would improve. Examples might include the following:

- To reduce blurting out comments in class without raising his hand
- To use the same book and be on the same page that the class is working on in large group activities
- To have no missing assignments at school

These target behaviors must be observable. You must be able to count them. They must be discrete, identifiable behaviors that everyone would agree upon by just looking at them. They should not be broad general references to attitudes, feelings or emotions. In the examples above, everyone can notice and count times when the student is blurting out comments, or being on the same page, or missing assignments. You have problems when your target behaviors are "to feel better about himself," "to try harder," "to have better self-esteem," "to like school more," or "to be a happier person." These are wonderful goals, but they cannot be measured. Instead, ask yourself what the subject would look like if he felt better about himself. Translate that feeling into observable behaviors. Does he volunteer more? Does he try harder by spending more time in his books? Does he bring up in conversation good school experiences at home? Is he seen smiling spontaneously more of the day?

We usually select the one or two target behaviors that everyone regards as the most troublesome. This is not hard to do. I have found that parents can identify these fairly quickly, even if they cannot translate them into observable, measurable behaviors as easily.

Measurable Baseline

Before any treatment is started, you should have a clear knowledge of the extent of the symptoms for which you are seeking treatment. There should be a clear, quantifiable, measure of frequency, intensity, and duration. Wodrich and Kush [1998] show how this is possible with existing questionnaires. This might be available from the initial evaluation and diagnosis, but it may not be spelled out in the evaluation sufficiently to use as baseline data.

Taking the time to establish a baseline is essential. This enables you to form accurate opinions about whether an intervention is working. If there is progress it will give you cause for hope and celebration even if there are still some symptoms present. I have seen students who were acting out 20 times a day who, with the help of some intervention, were able to reduce that to three times a day. It seems clear when you hear those numbers that some real progress has been made; but without those numbers, a parent may not perceive any progress at all because he or she is still coping with acting out three times a day. Without knowing concretely that this frequency has moved from 20 to three, they may be too close to the situation to recognize the improvement at all.

The same can be seen for intensity and duration. Episodes of acting out may have involved breaking personal property and initially endangering the safety of those around them. The acting out may have been reduced to just screaming with little or no physical damage. While this seems like improvement, without measuring it, the episodes of screaming will still be upsetting. Finally, a temper tantrum might have lasted two hours initially and with treatment it might be reduced to 15 minutes. The same applies here.

Get the Opinions of Others

Because of the blind spots I mentioned earlier, it is helpful to get some measure of these behaviors from others. There are rating forms available from many source, which also include forms for adults. I believe that it is important to form opinions about progress on the target behaviors on the basis of objective outside data, as much or more as on the basis of our own observations. It is also helpful when others volunteer information that is not specifically asked for.

For example, if you ask an outside observer, who is in a position to observe the individual receiving the treatment, whether he or she has noticed that the individual is better at not interrupting others, that person will have at least a subtle pressure to confirm what you are asking about. (Lawyers call this "leading the witness.") If, however, you ask that same person if they have noticed anything different about the person in question and they volunteer comments about the target behaviors, you can feel more confident about that data. Of course we all want to hear encouraging news, but we must resist the temptation to influence the outcome of the measurement if we are to expect the information to drive treatments that will be of genuine help.

Keep a Daily Log

Finally, it is helpful to keep some kind of daily log about your experiences with the various treatments. These do not have to be elaborate, but they should include dates and times. There will be times when you will note reactions that were not anticipated. There may be some pleasant surprises that might go unnoticed without this kind of observation.

CHAPTER ELEVEN

. . . .

Sample Behavior Modification Plans

TWO OF THE MOST commonly heard complaints with attention-deficit/ hyperactivity disorder (ADHD) are that students do not hand in assignments, or they rush through them just to get them finished. In this chapter, I shall give specific behavior modification plans to address these two problems.

Sample Behavior Plan #1

On page 80 we see a behavior plan for Johnny. He was not turning in any homework, even though his parents closely supervised him at home and helped him tuck it into his notebook before he left for school. Let us examine the plan.

TARGET BEHAVIOR

The target behavior is brief and to the point. It is clear, it can be measured, and it is true. Notice that there is no moralizing. No effort has been made to explain why. Those are distractions. Keep this document clean and focused.

THE PLAN

The parents should buy a package of 3" x 5" cards and write the date of the school days for the next few weeks in an upper corner of the card. They should ask Johnny's teacher to keep track of whether he hands in

Behavior Modification Plan: Sample #1

Target behavior:

not turning in homework

The plan:

give teacher some 3x5 cards, pre-dated. ask teacher to put a Y or N on them with her initials, daily   Y = all assignments turned in   N = one or more missing

Contracted reward:

When Johnny brings home a Y he gets all standard privileges

Contracted punishment:

When Johnny brings home an N, he loses video games, TV, bedtime snack

Evaluate the contract:

in 5 school days

Signatures: *mom, dad, Johnny*

assignments or not for each day and simply write a "Y" or an "N" on the card and then write her initials to ensure that she, in fact, wrote the note.

A "Y" means that Johnny handed in every assignment. An "N" means that there was at least one missing. Notice that you are not asking the teacher to count how many were missing, score them in advance, or give you a percentage of missing assignments. I do not think it is fair to ask the teacher to do that much recordkeeping on a daily or regular basis. It is not necessary. The standard in this plan is that ALL assignments must be turned in.

CONTRACTED REWARD/PUNISHMENT

Notice that this plan considers the standard privileges of TV, video games, and bedtime snacks as rewards. In many homes, children have the feeling that these are federally guaranteed rights. Removing them is grounds for filing a complaint with the local children's services board. In fact, love, food, shelter, and clothing are rights. The absence of these is grounds for abuse or neglect. Beyond that, children need to earn privileges.

In too many homes, children are given everything. Then, when behavior specialists talk about rewards, parents panic and wonder how much more this is going to cost. (This is not only true with wealthy private clients. I taught a parenting class primarily for Medicaid families and told parents that they need to take away TV, a specific brand name of video games, and bedtime snacks, and one parent asked if he should take away a second specific video game also. His child had both. He was not trying to be cute. This represents the difficulties some families have in comprehending a system of rewards and punishments.)

This plan will work for most children. If you have a particularly stubborn situation, or if it has gone on for some time, you may need to plug in some additional rewards, as we shall see in the next example.

EVALUATE THE CONTRACT

It may be that this plan will not work without adding an additional reward. That is what will be assessed during the time when you evaluate the contract. This plan indicates that you will evaluate it in five school days. This is good to see if there is something wrong, but do not be surprised if nothing right happens yet. Remember that sometimes students do not respond for a while, hoping that parents will give up on the plan.

Expect to stick to the plan for another five school days, and another. This may take some time. On the other hand, this plan may start working well almost immediately. When it does start working well, you may wish to consider a slightly more private way of getting this information. You may modify the plan to have the student note when he has completed all assignments and keep track of his own successes.

The ultimate goal is to have the individual carry out these management strategies privately. It is clear that people with ADHD need these kinds of concrete management techniques, but people usually evolve their own sets of strategies as they mature and are able to take more responsibility themselves.

SIGNATURES

The step involving signatures is designed to ensure that everyone had some influence on the plan. Just what this involvement for children looks like is marvelously spelled out in Chapter 5 of the book: *The Parent's Handbook Systematic Training For Effective Parenting*, by Dinkmeyer, McKay, and Dinkmeyer. This is not the primary purpose for this book, but when children have authentic influence in the plan that is used, they feel more ownership of the plan and are more inclined to participate with it and make it work.

Sample Behavior Plan #2

Page 83 shows an example of a plan for another common problem with ADHD students. The child does not work at an even level of effort for an entire assignment. It seems like she satisfies herself that she can do the first two or three items and then dashes off guesses at the rest.

Behavior Modification Plan: Sample #2

Target behavior: doing the first half of an assignment well, then missing most of the rest.

The plan: Divide every assignment page in half. Calculate the percentage right in the first half and the second half.

Contracted reward: When second half is not lower than the first half, Susie gets a sticker, and 5 stickers can be traded in for a trip to the toy store

Contracted punishment: When the second half is lower than the first, Susie loses TV privileges for that night

Evaluate the contract: in 5 school days

Signatures: Mom, Dad, Susie

TARGET BEHAVIOR

This example defines the problem, again, without any speculation as to what is causing it. It might be tempting to write that she rushes through the rest, but that is not certain. She may sit over problems for a long time, but give them little thought. It might be tempting to write that she does not care about the rest, but that is probably not true and certainly not necessary for the purpose of a behavior plan. So keep these target behaviors clear, brief, and descriptive.

THE PLAN

This plan involves a little work for the parents. They must count the total number of problems or tasks on a page. Then they divide that in half and see how many were right on the first half and how many were right on the second half. If the second half has fewer right than the first half, the contracted punishment takes place. If the second half has the same number or more right than the first half, the contracted reward is carried out.

If there is an odd number of tasks on a page, you are going to have to round off the number somehow. You may give the student the benefit of rounding one problem in their favor, but do not get caught up in arguments about bending the rule for just one more problem beyond that. Efforts by students to get parents to bend the rules ultimately threaten the very power of the plan and, therefore, how quickly it will improve the behavior of the student.

The other sections are similar to the first plan.

Summary

Implementing these plans comes naturally for some parents. For other parents, this process is awkward, stilted, and unnatural. If you find the process unnatural and hard to comprehend, take the time to study parenting manuals that cover this much more carefully. This is not the whole of parenting, but it is a necessary part. If you lack the skills to do this, you are at a serious disadvantage for being a successful parent.

CHAPTER TWELVE

. . . .

Strategies for Home and School

THERE ARE STRATEGIES that have proven to be helpful in working with people with attention-deficit/hyperactivity disorder (ADHD). Parents, teachers, and employers can learn these and use them, even if they do not understand exactly why they work. Anhalt and colleagues [1998] report on a "kit" of interventions that includes consequences for appropriate behavior, consequences for inappropriate behavior, and peer-mediated interventions:

> The basis of the program is that groups of children try to follow the class rules and instructions in exchange for the privilege to play the Rewards Target Game (RTG). Groups of children receive happy faces for following classroom rules and teacher instructions. Teachers are encouraged to provide enthusiastic labeled praises to individual and groups of children as often as possible, particularly when giving happy faces to a group.
>
> For instances of noncompliant and disruptive behavior, groups receive sad faces. However, children have the opportunity to modify their behavior before earning a sad face. This opportunity is given through a visual warning signal. [Anhalt et al. 1998, p. 68]

These can be used immediately while you are still trying to get your arms around the new learnings of behavior modification.

Large-scale studies clearly point to "behavior modification, however, as being more effective than cognitive or cognitive-behavioral strategies in enhancing behavior control in this population" [DuPaul & Eckert 1997, p. 22]. There are sound behavioral reasons why these work, but you do not have to know them to use them. Let us plunge right in, then, so that you can experience a certain measure of improvement immediately.

Front-Load Instructions

Have you ever noticed that authority figures like parents or teachers will spend one or two sentences giving instructions, but will spend 10 or 15 sentences harping when the person fails to do any or all parts of the instructions? This is just backwards.

Caregivers would find more success if they devoted more time to planning what they want to do up front and repeating the conditions in careful and thorough instructions. Of course, they will have to do this over the objections of the child, himself. The child will quickly jump to the belief that he understands what is being asked. He will indicate that he's got it. He will wriggle around and act like he is in great pain while hearing the instructions. He will, however, be more likely to remember the details if they have been rehearsed in his ear a few times before beginning.

My father seemed to have discovered this secret when I was young. He would call it, "making the plan." I used to hate these planning sessions. It seemed like he was wearing out the plan we were going to follow. At the same time, when we did follow the plan, I was able to contribute smoothly to the work because of all this advanced planning. We relied less upon my paying attention to instructions during the carrying out of the plan, because I had been briefed on what we were going to do before the plan was started. This process of planning in advance did make some of the most elaborate projects possible for me. I was able to contribute meaningfully on some pretty "grown-up" ac-

tivities in this way—a source of pride to me then, and a material benefit to my father.

"Chunk" Instructions

It seems obvious that if a child has difficulty remembering the details
of verbal directions, those verbal directions should contain as few details as possible. Put the details into chunks, with each chunk contain-
ing only those items needed to finish that part. For example, instead of
telling a child to do all the odd numbered problems in Section A, and
all odd and even problems in Section B, and only every third problem
in Section C, break this up into three separate chunks. Tell the child to
do all the odd numbered problems in Section A and come back up to
see you. Then examine her work and, if successful, go on to all items in
Section B, and so on.

This strategy has several advantages. It will require the student to
remember only what is essential for that part of the assignment. It will
provide the teacher with more opportunities to encourage the student
for successful compliance. Finally, it will allow the student to get up
and move around the room more. This is something the child generally welcomes. Whether she wants to see the teacher that often is not
clear; but she seems to appreciate a certain amount of gross motor
stimulation.

When I do classroom observations, I often see a teacher hand out
six pages of worksheets, covering several different subjects. The teacher
will give the students prolonged instructions about each one with the
expectation that the student will then be busy with desk work while the
teacher is doing small group instruction. The motive of having students busy at the same time the teacher is doing small group instruction is great. I suspect, however, that this is not developmentally appropriate for many younger students, and I know it is out of the question for a child with ADHD.

There can be different kinds of chunks within one section. Instead of telling a student to underline all the subjects and circle all the predicates, make this two separate chunks, even though it involves the same section of sentences.

Some students discover this strategy for themselves. I saw an 8-year-old boy who had much difficulty remembering the different parts of a written assignment. His solution was to write down all the words first. Then he would go through the entire assignment and erase the letters that were first written in lower case to apply all the capitalization rules. Then he would go over the entire assignment again working on only one kind of punctuation rule at a time. This process is painfully slow, but he had developed it to ensure that he did not overlook elements that needed to be done, even though he did not trust his ability to remember them all together.

Mnemonic Devices

A mnemonic device is some kind of trick or gimmick to help you remember things. When instructions cannot be chunked, mnemonic devices can be used to ensure that the child will remember all the parts. Mnemonic devices are most effective if they are dramatic, silly, outrageous, or humorous.

For example, if a student has homework in English, math, and science, he obviously needs to remember these three books in those critical few seconds when he is running to his locker or desk in a mad dash to go home. Even after a full day of activities he is expected to remember these three assignments. This is extremely unlikely.

One feature of individuals with ADHD is that they frequently are lost in thought about other things. Sometimes they worry about things that don't matter. These students often worry so much about how to avoid a long line leaving school that, as they are stuffing things into their locker and pulling out their coat, they are planning their route to get out instead of rehearsing the events of the day and what assignments they may have. This feature of missing what they are supposed to remember because they are worried about an immediate problem is quite common for children with ADHD.

The student with ADHD may find it helpful to use the first letter of each of these three subject areas: "E" for English "M" for math, and "S" for science and put them together to make a "word" that will help him remember them. He should do this rehearsal some minutes before the final bell rings. He may form the *word* MES and tell himself that he has to bring a "MES" home from school tonight. He may find it easier to remember the colors of the book jackets. For example, it may be easier to remember: two yellows and a red. Then, at his locker or desk, he only needs a second to remember what this means, but the prompt to remember all three is there.

Keep in mind what powerful forces you are trying to overcome with this strategy. You are expecting a student who normally slams a locker shut and runs, to use these strategies in those critical few seconds. You are expecting him to think about homework, which is not popular in the first place. The student may need to build this mnemonic device over the day. He is not likely to create the device after the final bell. It is also unlikely that students under 12 will have much success with this at all, but it may be useful for younger children with the prompting of a teacher.

Frequent Prompts

Students can know what they are supposed to do but drift off that purpose in their own thoughts. These students find it helpful to have frequent prompts or reminders if these prompts meet certain criteria. Of course, students do not like a shrill haranguing every time they are caught off task. They have received many of these in the past and are easily upset by them.

They do find gentle, subtle cues helpful. A student and a teacher can have a private plan where some code phrase, word, or number will represent an entire packet of instructions. For example, when the teacher notices that the student has drifted off task in his own thoughts, the teacher could say, "Twelve makes a dozen." This could prompt the student that he was dozing, and that he needs to get back on task.

This prompt could be shorter, like "twelve." It may be more effective if this prompt creates a mental picture. The expression, "mantis" may be understood by both the student and teacher to represent the kind of alertness and focus that the insect uses when about to eat another insect. This combines the basic prompt with a vivid mental image that would further improve the student's ability to do the desired task.

Having these prompts understood and established well in advance will give the teacher, or caregiver, additional long distance ways of prompting without always needing to be by the student's side. Some teachers also like to walk around the room and gently touch the student on the shoulder when they notice that he is off task. If done in a subtle way, this often does not offend the student, but rather helps him get back on the job.

There are electronic training devices that work powerfully in this same way. I'm thinking of one developed by Michael Gordon, and I believe is available for purchase. The teacher is equipped with a button clipped to his belt. When the teacher observes that the student is off task, he pushes the button. This signal does two things. It lights a small red light bulb on a box on the student's desk for a few seconds, and it deducts a certain preassigned number of points from a total that had been accumulating on a digital screen on the same box. This cleverly provides a quick visual prompt for being off task, and gives the student an immediate way of evaluating himself for how often this has happened by seeing how much it has cost him.

The student could tape a picture of an owl or a mantis on his desk, or keep one in his notebook. This image will help prompt him to stay focused. This is something that he can do for himself.

One helpful book, *Becoming a Master Student,* by David B. Ellis, suggests using the phrase "I am here now" whenever the student notices himself drifting off task. This is easier for older students to do. The problem with younger students is that they do not notice when they are off task. From age 12 upward, however, this self-statement can be somewhat helpful if the student uses it regularly.

Consider this real-life illustration. I once had a 9-year-old girl brought to my office because she had tremendous problems with getting work done in a timely manner. The parents reported that she would take two hours at night and only get two math problems done. I used this "I am here now" strategy with her. Because of her age, it had to be coupled with a system to ensure that she would remember to use it. We made a rule that every time she wrote down the number of the problem on her paper, she would use that as a prompt to say "I am here now" to herself. That is, when she started on her math homework, she would write down the number of the first problem "1" and then say, "I am here now" to herself. Then she would solve that problem and then write "2," which prompted her to say, "I am here now." again, and go on to solve the second problem. If she had 20 math problems, she had to say "I am here now" for each problem. Her parents returned the next week reporting that with this plan she was able to get all but two of her math problems done in school.

Prompts work because they are brief, not aversive, and helpful. They need to represent a lot of thought or instruction, but not be long themselves. They need to be friendly in tone.

The research on teaching individuals to prompt themselves with some kind of self-statement is not as strong as I would like to see [Abikoff 1991], so I would not suggest placing too much reliance on this. To the extent that it approaches the rules for a good behavior modification program, it will be more powerful. Some students, however, seem to like to have something that they can do for themselves like this to help.

Coaching is a term for having someone other than the individual provide these prompts. Ratey, Hallowel, and Miller [1997] provide an excellent description of this form of psychosocial help. A coach can be anyone from a friend to a professional coach. The coach notices when the person drifts off task, or becomes less productive, and provides cues to correct the situation. The coach compensates for weaknesses in the individual's executive functioning of planning, organizing, and attending. Or, as these authors put it, "A coach acts as a kind of neurocognitive prosthetic device, assisting the ADHD adult to compensate for the deficiencies in their executive functions that impede their ability to plan, organize, and monitor behavior."

Shapiro [1995] addresses the peculiar stubbornness of ADHD patients to respond to cognitive-behavioral approaches with a refinement based upon quite a bit of teaching, self-management, and self-rating. He reports success with more than 20 middle-school students. This plan used a successful contingency management strategy: where there is a lot of scoring, the scoring is done frequently—every 10 or 15 minutes—and the scores are shared and discussed with the student frequently and regularly. These details seem to be the strength of psychosocial interventions, lots of charting, a clear understanding of what the charts mean, which understanding is frequently rehearsed, and the time between assessment or charting is brief.

Routines

The popular television program, "Mr. Rogers' Neighborhood" has modeled an effective strategy for parents and children, something that few parents fully use. The opening of every program is always the same. Mr. Rogers comes in, changes his shoes, hangs up his jacket, and puts on a sweater. This is a routine. He does it every time.

Some mechanics use a routine in laying out their tools before they get started on a job. They methodically lay out their tools in the same arrangement every time. In this way they can reach over and grab a tool without looking and expect that tool to be there.

These routines help people remember the various elements of a task and help them notice if something is missing. If, for example, the mechanic in the above illustration always lays out his tools in the same order each time, he will quickly notice if one of his tools is missing. There will be a gap where a tool was supposed to be. This creates a visual prompt to look for that tool.

If you want a child to hang up his coat and put away his shoes upon entering the house, you could make this a routine. Get a red-colored hanger, put a red dot above the bar where you want the hanger to be placed, and cut out two red forms the shape of his shoes for the floor of the closet where you want him to put his shoes. You can cover the forms with clear contact paper so that water won't destroy them too quickly.

Walk the child through this routine a few times so that it becomes as automatic as it is for Mr. Rogers. Then reward him for doing it a few more times. Eventually this will settle in as a routine that needs little management.

I have a huge briefcase that I use to carry around test kits. I move around from school to school, setting up for testing in all of these places. I have a contract with the Department of Youth Services in a facility more than 20 miles from my office. I do testing in schools nearly 30 miles from my office in the opposite direction. If I left a stop watch, or a file with blank test protocols at one location, I would be in deep trouble trying to test at another location 50 miles away.

My safeguard is to put everything back into my briefcase in exactly the same order every time. This has become so habitual that my briefcase has taken on a particular "look" when everything is in its right spot. I have seen this image so often that when I forget something, it does not look right even on a quick glance. When the configuration in the briefcase does not look quite right, a quick scan around the desk area where I was working will reveal the missing element. This routine has proven to be invaluable over the years.

If a student always stacked his books in his book bag in exactly the same order, with the notebook on the bottom, and other items always in their exact place, he would be able to see quickly if there was something missing in much the same way.

Work with Strengths

My briefcase method, unlike mnemonic devices, relies heavily upon good visual discrimination. You have to look to the individual's test results to see how adequate the child's visual perception is before you relied heavily upon this kind of intervention. Some of the mnemonic strategies I described earlier rely more heavily upon verbal comprehension. Again, test results should be able to tell you how likely those strategies are to succeed with any particular individual.

This gives us a glimpse about how you can use test results for more than a careful diagnosis. Test results give us valuable information about what modalities might be helpful to use. Even more importantly, if testing finds weaknesses in some cognitive modalities, those results can give us valuable information about what areas to avoid when suggesting interventions.

Our memories can be prompted by all the senses. I have found it useful to deliberately tap my jacket pocket to both feel the presence of my car keys and hear the jingle of them in my pocket before shutting my car door after I have locked it. This little ritual, which is a combination of motor and auditory sensations, has been helpful in preventing me from locking my keys in the car many times.

Opportunities for Great Creativity

One of the most common descriptors we hear about individuals with ADHD is "rapid boredom." One avenue of relief is in these various gimmicks that people discover to overcome problems that they iden-tify. This is an area for great creativity.

There was an effect that they used to talk about frequently in intro-ductory Psychology courses, called the "Hawthorne effect." This sug-gested that any intervention was likely to produce the desired outcome at least initially. It was only after the newness wore off that the desired outcome would vanish.

Researchers who did not understand this effect and only conducted their research for short interventions were always showing positive outcomes. It was only when people began asking about how long the benefits continued that some disappointing results were experienced.

This might be why a teacher who continuously introduces new things, and who is constantly changing some of the conditions in the class-room has more student attention. This teacher is taking advantage of this effect. This teacher is combating, to some degree, the ravages of rapid boredom. This should not be confused with a teacher who has unpredictable rules. Frequent change can occur with structure. The structure refers to how clearly the changes are communicated, and how consistently they are enforced, not how long they last.

Chapter Thirteen

• •

My Experience: How an Adult Decides to Treat ADHD

Halfway through writing this book, a newspaper article persuaded me to pursue a formal diagnosis of attention-deficit/hyperactivity disorder (ADHD) for myself and to try a medical intervention. I had been aggressively diagnosing ADHD in children and adults for 12 years. Early in that 12-year experience I became convinced that I had attention-deficit/hyperactivity disorder, predominantly inattentive subtype, but I was not interested in doing anything more heroic about it than developing my own strategies that worked for me. I would like to share why I changed my mind.

When I was in the first grade I was the absolute lowest reader in the lowest reading group. If schools had as many school psychologists in the late 1950s as they do today, I might have been identified as learning disabled and accommodated into oblivion. Instead, I had a loving aunt who worked hard with me and got me propped up enough to pass.

My parents were loving, caring, and involved and did whatever they knew to do back then. I remember doing endless pages of "M's and N's," something my father recommended from his avocational studies as a graphoanalyst. He was an efficiency engineer by trade. "M's and N's" were rows of zig zags across each line for the entire page. They were supposed to make me both analytical and investigative. They probably worked.

All of the experiences related in the first chapter of this book were my own. In those experiences, with the delays in reading and these "M's and N's," I had little evidence of any remarkable intelligence in my young years. When I look back on my early years now, I see some unusual signs of intelligence. I remember sharing several ideas for inventions with my father, only to have him tell me that they already existed. My mother gave me five books by Sigmund Freud when I was 11 or 12 and I was captivated by his long sentences (or A. A. Brill's long sentences, since they were in English), and I did enjoy *The Interpretation of Dreams*. I edited a German newsletter in junior high, which might have signaled some intelligence, but I was also capable of some incredible lapses that gave my father at least as much cause for concern.

Throughout junior and senior high, I seemed to be able to get high average grades without cracking a book, but I had great difficulty sustaining my attention on studying in order to push those grades any higher. I was interested in Psychiatry and started at the Ohio State University in pre-med. The demands for attention soon got me to shift my major to Elementary Education. I taught for one year after graduating and then was accepted at Teachers College, Columbia University in a master's program in Educational Psychology.

I moved back to Ohio after receiving the master's degree and had to take additional graduate course work in School Psychology to get certificated in the State of Ohio to practice as a school psychologist. I worked as a school psychologist for the necessary number of years in order to take the state licensure exam. I had to take one part twice before passing and became licensed to practice in the State of Ohio.

I immediately set up a private practice, in addition to holding a contract with a public school district. I am by nature an ambitious person. Perhaps as some kind of accommodation to my ADHD, I have always liked having a lot of irons in the fire. That way I can move from one to another when I get bored with one—I do get bored rather rapidly. In this manner of working, however, I have been quite productive.

I have worked on many committees, I have published articles in professional and religious magazines, I have edited my own church's national publication for 19 years, I headed a committee that developed Sunday school lessons, and I have rewritten a 450-page novel five times. I wrote a workbook on pastoral counseling and traveled around North America training our clergy on its use; not to mention testing and writing reports on zillions of individuals between my public and private work. None of this would be possible without a wife who handles essentially everything around the house, and three obedient children who help too.

I run through this list of accomplishments to give the reader the impression that I have been productive; however, I feel that I have had to work hard and sustain a high level of motivation across an array of works in order to do that.

Colleagues have urged me to do something more aggressively about my ADHD for years. One colleague had a husband who began taking Ritalin, and she reported that he was much more alert and felt that he was much more powerful at getting paperwork done in a timely manner. She urged me to at least try Ritalin to see if I would not also experience these benefits.

My answer was always the same. I was fairly certain that Ritalin would make a significant improvement in my work, and I was afraid that it would work so well that I would never want to stop taking it.

After ignoring more than a year of this kind of prompting, I read an Associated Press article in the local paper on adults with ADHD. If it had been written locally, the paper would likely have contacted me for a quote. After all, I forgot to mention that I wrote a column for them for one year. This AP article quoted a man my age, 44, as saying that he felt that he could do two or three times his usual work with 80% of the effort when he started taking Ritalin. That sold me.

Also about this same time, my family went to a tennis tournament in Cincinnati. My wife informed me that we had agreed to meet at the main gate when the tournament was over. We walked out separately, because the children wanted to get autographs from the players, and she wanted to get something to drink. I had not attended to this verbal agreement and could not find her outside another gate, which greatly delayed the time we finally left, and we were both angry at the misunderstanding. This inattention to details was the final straw.

I called a local psychiatrist whom I had met professionally and genuinely respected. He was guarded at first because he kindly shared that he felt that I was quite productive, having made a reasonable reputation for myself in the same community. He informed me that a famous artist used amphetamines daily to make himself more productive and was concerned that I was unwittingly doing the same.

I appreciated his caution. ADHD is, after all, something of a fad disorder and considerable clinical care should be used in identification, as already discussed in Chapter 2. I related my past experiences and how long I had resisted before taking this step. I further had a list of highly specific symptoms that I would try to observe objectively. This preparation impressed him and he gave me a 30-day trial prescription for Ritalin.

I watched for these specific symptoms: 1) increased facility at vocabulary and proper name retrieval in conversation and speaking, 2) improved attention to verbal instructions from my wife and others, 3) staying attentive in conversations long enough to complete sentences, and 4) increased length of sustained attention on paper work at a desk. These seemed to be the areas where I was experiencing the greatest difficulty. Let me elaborate somewhat, one at a time.

When I talked with others, I seemed to have moments when I blocked on a specific vocabulary word or a proper name. This appeared to be happening more often than is normal. I frequently halted and asked someone else for the specific term I was struggling to retrieve.

My wife repeatedly complained about my difficulties hearing specifics of comments or requests that she made. Later, when it was obvious that I had missed the item she mentioned, she called this to my attention and I had no recollection of ever hearing it.

The amazing thing was that I only missed the first five or six words. It was as if there was a delay in my ability to shift focus from what I was thinking about when someone around me began speaking to me. From about the sixth or seventh word onward I heard everything they said. If some of those first six words were crucial, I was in trouble.

I told people around me that it helped if they put some preamble in front of their first sentence like: "Well, Paul, I'm going to tell you this ... " This would give me the time I needed to shift attention and I would not have to ask them to repeat themselves. Instead, most people began by saying: "Take these keys to the office and wait there in case they have something to send back." I would hear, "Wait there in case they have something to send back." Perhaps I'd even start toward the office being faintly aware of that word as I was shifting my attention only to get scolded for not picking up the keys that they were holding in their outstretched hand.

I had an unnerving habit—a humorous habit to my children—of beginning a sentence and somewhere in the middle of the sentence I became distracted by other thoughts or observations and stopped talking, leaving the rest of the sentence unspoken. This habit caused many around me to actually finish the sentences for me.

Finally, I felt that I could only remain at my desk working on sustained paperwork for perhaps a half hour. At that point I would have to get up and move around. I got a drink, I moved something around, I did anything else just to break up what was becoming a boring activity. This would, obviously, limit my productivity. This is where the strategy of having "many balls in the air at one time" became helpful. When I became bored with one, I could jump over and do another. Then I jumped back and forth, pushing all my projects toward completion a little bit at a time. The first three target symptoms gave me the look of the "absent-minded professor." The last genuinely limited my productivity.

On September 4, 1995, I took my first 10 milligrams of Ritalin. I quickly settled into a regimen of taking 10 milligrams of Ritalin three times a day: 7:30 A.M., 11:00 A.M., and 3:00 P.M.

Side Effects

In my intense scrutiny of the first few days, I thought I noticed the following "side effects." I felt that I slept much lighter, dramatically so if I took the medication after 4:00 P.M. I felt a slight diminution in appetite. I felt a sensation like a golf ball resting on the top of my stomach. I had a slight saline taste in my mouth. Finally, I had the slightest feeling of light-headedness, but this might have been alertness.

After a few weeks, all of these side effects disappeared except the difficulty in falling asleep if I took the medication after 4:00 P.M.

Benefits

The benefits were exactly as expected. Those around me agreed that I completed sentences better, I attended to the details of verbal directions better, I retrieved vocabulary words and proper names better, and I seemed a little more aggressive about picking up the next stack of paperwork, rather than seeking ways of escape.

Assessing benefits of a medication is a tricky business. I was aware that I was highly motivated to believe that the medication worked. I know enough about human behavior to know that a person is capable of producing those effects in the short run just from internal motivation, and could do so on a placebo, or powerless prescription.

I was more than satisfied, but I felt that I needed more objective data. I asked people I worked with whether they saw any benefits. They generally said yes, and those that were in a position to know about the more specific target behaviors I was shooting for also confirmed improvements there. There remained no question in my mind after I had two unexpected experiences.

I was sitting in a restaurant having lunch with a colleague from work. It was about 12:00 noon so the second pill, taken at 11:00 A.M., should be well into its most effective stages. This was several weeks after the initial excitement. I noticed to my great chagrin that I was having genuine difficulties retrieving certain vocabulary and names. I was deeply saddened by this because I had held such great excitement for how this very feature had been helped by the medication.

I had a genuine feeling of grieving because I was being faced with some irrefutable data that I was not remembering certain vocabulary and names in spite of being on the medication. Then I tapped my shirt pocket. I noticed that there were still two pills there. Every morning I put three pills in my shirt pocket. I take one at 7:30 A.M. while driving to work. I take the second at 11:00 A.M. At 12:00 noon, there should have only been one pill left in that pocket. I then realized that I had forgotten to take the 11:00 A.M. pill. I was delighted with this discovery because I considered it to be a more objective assessment. I was willing to admit that the medication was not working, until I learned that I was not on the medication.

The second experience was on a family trip to Canada. During this visit I experienced a tremendous benefit that I had not identified as a target behavior goal for the medication. I had taken along a book about scoring the Minnesota Multiphasic Personality Inventory for Adolescents. I wanted to read sections of it on the trip. I asked my wife to drive and I started to look at the book. After some time I became aware that I was going through a great deal of the book with ease in spite of the usual noise from my three sons in the back of the van.

It occurred to me that on previous long van trips I had tried to read books as well, but threw the book down on the floor of the van within

15 minutes because I could not tune out the background noise of the boys in the van. Previously with that kind of background noise I would re-read a sentence perhaps six or eight times before I could attend to what that one sentence said, but I would forget the context of the rest of the paragraph. It was simply impossible for me to read a book while traveling with all the noise of a typical trip.

This was an unexpected benefit. I had not listed it as a target goal for the medication. I was, however, completely delighted with this discovery. This represents a bonus that I had not thought of. I cannot describe the sense of celebration that I had in suddenly being able to do something that was previously not possible for me.

At this point, I have no plans to increase the dosage to 20 milligrams three times a day. It is my understanding that you do not become accustomed to Ritalin, or develop a tolerance to it that would require periodic increases. It may be possible that my attention would increase even more with an increase in dosage; but I am satisfied with the response at this level. I, like all patients I guess, am interested in the maximum benefit with the lowest possible dosage. I believe that I am at that point.

I would have to say from my personal experience that Ritalin does not hit you like an afterburner on a jet, or a turbo charger on a sports car engine. It is more subtle than that. It appears to quietly, gently, boost your motivation to focus on desired tasks. Whether those tasks are verbal conversations, reading, or writing, Ritalin appears to increase your ability to stay on that one, single, job and not become bored as quickly as before.

Summary

I would say that my experience has several features that I would recommend for anyone pursuing a medical intervention for ADHD. Let me highlight them in the following sections so that they are clear to those who may be planning on pursuing a medical intervention for themselves. I will use the steps in measuring behavior that I discussed in Chapter 9.

BEGIN WITH A MEASURABLE BASELINE

I evaluated my list of symptoms and attached some real numbers to them. I was able to tolerate desk work for about a half hour before I became restless. My difficulty in retrieving specific vocabulary occurred during nearly every conversation that lasted more than two minutes. I missed details of verbal directions three or more times per day. I also began sentences and did not complete them during almost every conversation that lasted more than two minutes.

When I look back on these, I wonder at the patience of those around me. I must have had a reputation among my friends of appearing quite absent-minded. My friends and colleagues must have understood that they must accommodate for these symptoms in dealing with me. Perhaps some did not and did not remain friends or colleagues. Perhaps I was not selected for some jobs for these reasons.

IDENTIFY TARGET BEHAVIORS OR GOALS

I decided that I wanted to retrieve proper names and specific vocabulary in nearly every conversation with only rare exceptions—more like normal. I wanted to finish all my sentences in conversations with people. And I wanted to sit at my desk and work on paperwork for two hours before becoming restless.

GET THE OPINIONS OF OTHERS

I told some of my colleagues at work that I was taking Ritalin. I asked them generally if they noticed any changes in my behavior. I tried not to lead them into saying what I was looking for. I wanted them to volunteer comments about these target behaviors if they could do so honestly.

I think this is essential, because of our capacity to convince ourselves of nearly everything. The caution, however, is that the target is to get to normal. People will quickly see your behavior as normal, not different. They will forget what has been so unforgettable to you. As far as they care concerned, you are behaving in ways you should have all along. They will not see a need to celebrate like you will.

KEEP A DAILY LOG

I wrote down my impressions daily on a small notebook. This is the only reason that I can list the initial side effects and benefits so clearly. Your log will surprise you when you read it later. There will be specific observations that you will not remember making.

This log will also be quite helpful in communicating with your health care providers. This will convince them that you are thorough and objective.

Finally, temper your expectations with reality. When Ritalin works, it appears to "bump up" your motivation. It will not change grades from D's to A's by itself. Prospective patients should have this drummed into their heads. Too often the use of medication is oversold. Patients come to the office after early experiences with it believing that it met all their exaggerated claims. It is only months later when the newness wears off that there is a discouraging awareness that the medication is only one tool to help with these matters. This causes some to believe that the medication stopped working. The more likely explanation is that they overestimated what effect the medication was having, but that it *was* helping somewhat.

You will continue to need to value the goals you are seeking. You will need to continue to set more goals, milestones, and assert self-discipline to achieve those goals. These items are not supplanted by the medication. The medication merely allows you to be self-initiated, like everyone else, rather than start out in a hole in these important matters.

CHAPTER FOURTEEN

. . . .

Common Myths and Misunderstandings

THERE ARE SOME popular myths [DuPaul et al. 1997] that come up in discussions about attention-deficit/hyperactivity disorder (ADHD). Some are widely held and prevent some people from seeking help for their symptoms. I shall try to deal with some of the more common ones. It is critical to remember, however, that there are millions of people with ADHD and within that number there are bound to be unique individual responses. Generally, the following items are myths and should be properly understood.

Myth #1: Side Effects

Since up to 92% of people [Barkley 1994] properly identified with ADHD have a significant positive response to medication, this intervention is highly recommended. The question of side effects always comes up. After all, this is not a disorder for which just a short course of medication is recommended. It is likely to be at least for all the individual's school life, and maybe longer. Some of the medications most commonly associated with this disorder have been used for a long time. Longitudinal studies have come in showing them to be remarkably safe. Still, the decision about how safe is still up to the individuals or families dealing with the disorder.

I would worry about a parent that did not express concerns about side effects. These concerns must be balanced with a clear understanding of the effects of going through school without medication. What are the effects of being yelled at nearly every day, and having the other classmates laugh at you and feel that they can pile on with criticism when the teacher is mad at you? There are some individuals with severe cases of ADHD who simply will not get through a traditional educational setting without medication and psychosocial interventions. For these people, you cannot choose to have no side effects. You must choose the lesser of two "evils."

Myth #2: Medications Cause Tourette's Syndrome

There used to be a fear that some of the medications commonly used with ADHD might cause Tourette's syndrome in some individuals. It now appears that this was a mistake of coincidence instead of causality. The current explanation appears to be that when young people begin to develop the constellation of symptoms associated with Tourette's syndrome, these symptoms come on gradually. Early in that process schools or others are aggressively identifying the early symptoms as ADHD. Some of these were put on medications only to find that they continued developing the rest of the symptoms of Tourette's syndrome. People now believe that these individuals were going to have Tourette's syndrome whether any medication was used or not.

This is another place where the symptoms of ADHD are similar to the symptoms of many other disorders. It is fortunate that people are identifying these symptoms early and trying to do something about them. People just have to be prepared for those rare times when these early symptoms may be related to another disorder that is on the horizon.

This is probably related to what is going on in the next common misunderstanding that we will discuss.

Myth #3: Medications Stop Working

There are families who will report that a medication seemed to work fine for a while but that it just stopped working suddenly. They may go back to their health professional and begin on a different medication with positive reports again.

It seems rare that one of the traditional medications that was designed to modify one portion of the brain would work for a while and then stop working. There might be some reorganizing of the brain going on, or some other organic changes occurring, but what is more likely is that other disorders may be coming and going in the person.

No one believes that if they have a cold they cannot also have another illness. It is the same with ADHD. There is a growing conviction in professionals that it not only can exist with other disorders, but that this comorbidity may be common. What might be happening is that, through an individual's lifespan, he or she may have other disorders, such as adjustment disorder with anxiety. This can create the symptoms of ADHD in anyone for the length of time that the anxiety is present. In this case, it is not that the medication has stopped working. It is that another concern has developed for which other interventions will also be necessary.

So people going in with the report that the medication is no longer working may be placed on another kind of medication for these reasons without having this process fully explained to them. This is fine if they experience relief of the troubling symptoms, but it may be harmful if they are sharing misinformation about their experience with the best of intentions.

Myth #4: Medications Solve Your Problems

Some people look to medications for the complete solution. They feel that starting a medication will take care of the problem and they can go off to worry about other things. This is particularly true for families who are rushed, with many other irons in the fire. It should be understood that medication will improve the person's tolerance for tasks requiring sustained mental effort, it will tend to boost motivation somewhat, and it will increase the person's ability to focus on tasks. Most people still have to overcome a history of frustrations and bad habits that they have learned because of their difficulties. These are best attacked through the behavior modification strategies discussed in Chapters 8 and 9. The most successful treatment of ADHD combines these two major intervention categories: medication and behavior modification.

Myth #5: ADHD Goes Away at Puberty

The current view is that ADHD is a lifelong feature of one's cognitive makeup. It is commonly reported, however, that some of the hyperactive symptoms do seem to lessen during adolescence. This may be due to the child's growing awareness of time as he passes 12 years of age. He no longer regards the waiting period until the next break in the schedule, lunch, or physical activity to be an eternity beyond his ability to endure. He can now begin to monitor his own behavior, and he can begin to develop strategies of his own creation to help him control the hyperactive symptoms.

While this growing mental capacity to monitor his own behavior appears to help the hyperactive symptoms, it seems less successful with the inattentive symptoms. People do report some improvement in even the inattentive symptoms with the use of strategies like self-statements, metacognitions, or self-talk. This is different, of course, from the symptoms going away. They are just being handled more successfully by an individual as he grows through the various stages of cognitive development and gains the ability to pay attention to his own behaviors and thinking.

Myth #6: Just a Scheme to Make Psychologists Rich

This myth has caused me some soul searching. I have in the back of my mind the image of those so-called experts who recommended blood-letting to heal some diseases, or all those other horrors of ancient medical history. There is the faintest squeak of fear that 50 years from now books like this will be rendered laughable by what comes out later.

There is a difference between the kind of humility that jumps into action *now*, doing what you can to help with the knowledge that all is not known, and the kind of humility that waits on the side lines for additional information that will come down someday. I want to be on the side of those that sincerely try to help *now*, even if I will be corrected in some of the methodology some day. Perhaps the only saving difference might be the lack of arrogance.

I know that some of the medication interventions we are talking about seem to help. Whether all the explanations for why will be just as I have represented them here seems highly unlikely to me. I am making no claims for being a prophet. I am trying to be a helper who gets individuals successfully through educational and life challenges with the best of the known methods.

To those who say that ADHD does not exist, I say that a calendar year does not exist, either. It is an abstraction that we all agree to, based on some observations and definitions. We use calendar years for many important purposes in our lives, even though time could have been defined differently. We could have identified a year to be 730 days as easily as 365 days. It is helpful that we all simply agree on a common definition of a calendar year. It helps in communication around the world and in planning.

Likewise, it helps that we all agree on the cluster of symptoms that define ADHD, which helps in communicating and in planning. I hope that the definition will change and improve over the years. (It certainly has in the last 20 years.) I can easily see it being broken down into several disorders more clearly defined by brain location and function in the future.

Myth #7: ADHD Is Overidentified

You hear of schools where those in charge push many parents into getting stimulant medication for their children—as many as 50% of a school population. This does seem to be overidentification to me as well. I tend to agree with the estimate of 5%, or 1 in 20. In a survey of nurses, Bramlett and colleagues [1997] reported that 3% of the nurses' elementary population was on medication for ADHD. This is likely to be an underestimate since some only take medications at home, and some decline to take medications at all.

If 5% is the true incidence rate, let us look at that for a moment. Suppose you had a school psychologist in a district that either did not know about ADHD or did not believe in it. Suppose that person moved or retired. Suppose the new school psychologist is well-informed about this disorder. Suddenly, to the health professionals in that area, it is going to look like the school is overidentifying this disorder. Suddenly many parents are going to be approaching their doctors for some help with ADHD. Does this represent overidentification, or is the school finally identifying the proper percentage that they should have been identifying all along?

I obviously think the increase in this example is justified and proper. It makes me wonder what became of all the unidentified students in the earlier years. Did they drop out? Were they expelled? Did they make it through? You can guess about as well as I can. Some probably did make it through, those who had relatively milder cases, and/or those who had accommodating support from home, teachers, or friends.

If the incidence rate is truly 5%, then an elementary school of 300 students will have 15 students identified with ADHD. A high school of

3,000 students will have 150 students identified with ADHD. So do not get up in arms when you go to that high school of 3,000 students and someone tells you that there are 150 students there with ADHD. That is what is expected.

Murphy [1994] dealt with concerns that there may be increases in adults believing that they have ADHD, due to all the media attention it receives. He outlined evaluation safeguards that included documenting a lifelong trail of evidence of the symptoms, ruling out the contributions of other diagnoses, and establishing the presence of a significant impairment. Clearly, these precautions will help prevent false positives where ADHD is identified but does not really exist. Identification must be thorough, taking many factors into consideration.

Myth #8: Television and Video Games Cause ADHD

I have read this opinion in newspaper columns. I have heard it voiced by others. This is a difficult one. Since this disorder was around before television and video games, this cannot be exclusively true. I am not arrogant enough to say that it can never be true. I am not sure that enough is known about brain development to say that a heavy exposure to the features of television or video games cannot anatomically alter some brain systems at least slightly.

At the same time, there is the whole area of learned behavior. I do think there are students who are learning a powerful preference for rich, stimulating, and frequent rewards that are found on television and in video games particularly. Someone has called them "reinforcement junkies" meaning that they develop at least a strong preference—if not a need—for rich reinforcement schedules. That is, bells go off, lights flash, graphs change every few seconds to keep the individual constantly stimulated and attentive. If this is true, then this preference can be unlearned as well. A more appropriate intervention might be with behavior modification, such as removing those rich reinforcement schedules and creating additional reinforcements in and around school and work performance.

Tannock studied this commonly heard opinion and concluded the following:

> our findings confirm parents' observations that the children's ADHD symptoms are much less apparent when the child is engaged in motivating activities, such as television viewing and playing video games. On the other hand, the findings challenge the clinical assumption that the intrinsically motivating nature of these activities serves to normalize the children's behavior. Our findings indicated that children with ADHD remained more restless, inattentive, and talkative compared to normally developing peers, even during these highly motivating and preferred activities. [1997, p. 6]

These examiners learned during interviews with these parents after the research, that students with ADHD tended to play video games alone, and when they played with peers there was a common report that games were cut short with fights.

Myth #9: Sugar Can Cause ADHD Symptoms in Children

This opinion reflects a remarkable event in our culture. Rarely has a view been more widely held with no robust research support. Evidence of how widely this view is held is that it was used as a legal defense in a criminal trial, known as the "Twinkie defense." Wolraice and others [1995] conducted an exhaustive analysis of the literature and found no support for this view.

The fact that this view is so completely refuted, but still has such wide support, raises another question addressed by Hoover and Milich. This study looked at 35 boys between 5 and 7 years old who were identified by their mothers as "sugar sensitive." All of them were given a sugar substitute, but the mothers of some of them were told that their sons were given a high dose of sugar, and the mothers of others were told that they were given a sugar substitute. They found that

> Mothers who were told their children had ingested sugar rated their children as engaging in significantly more hyperactive behavior than did control mothers. These mothers acted on their expectancies by maintaining more physical proximity to their sons, giving more criticisms, and talking more frequently to them, in an apparently "hovering" or controlling manner. [Hoover & Milich 1994, pp. 510-511]

Myth #10: Children with ADHD Have Sleep Problems

Research since 1970 on sleep disturbances in children with ADHD was reviewed [Corkum et al. 1998], and that review generated more questions than answers. The authors summarized that children with ADHD were found to be more restless during sleep. They also noted that there was no difference, however, in total sleep time between children with ADHD and normal control groups depending upon medication regimen, etc.

Some studies they reviewed showed that ADHD children were rated as less rested after a night's sleep. There are enough clinical and anecdotal reports about parents' concerns about sleep that this area deserves additional attention. It, alone, does not appear to be a concern of such magnitude that it would outweigh many other considerations for seeking medical treatment for ADHD.

Conclusion

One of the motives for the rapid development of myths, and their abiding staying power in spite of the evidence, is our need to believe that we understand things that, maybe, we do not. We do not like to admit that we do not understand things. So we jump to conclusions that may meet the immediate facts, but do not hold up as true. These are myths.

If we could just deal with the present needs and facts we would be better off. We do not need to predict far into the future. We do not need to seek cause or blame. We need to support a person with some genuine differences in behavior and attention so that they can be successful too. If we only used the effort we spend on myths to make accommodations here and now, things would be much more successful.

CHAPTER FIFTEEN

· ·

Conclusion: When in Doubt, Err on the Side of Compassion

RICHTERS AND OTHERS [1995] conducted a selective review of the extant literature regarding many facets of attention-deficit/hyperactivity disorder (ADHD), including the effects of treatment. In spite of ADHD being a well-researched area, particularly for a childhood disorder, their review generated many questions. There are hints throughout the literature of subtypes in identification and subtypes of response to treatment [Rapport et al. 1994; Balthazor et al. 1991].

It has been remarkable to watch this field grow almost from year to year. As a practitioner to whom families come looking for answers, I am humbled to compare what is known now with what we were telling families as recently as five years ago. I certainly expect the next five years to bring an even greater percentage of growth in knowledge of this complicated set of symptoms called ADHD.

Still, a family with a 3-year-old now cannot wait until that child is 8 before we decide we know enough to act. We must act with what is known, and we must act compassionately with the humility to be teachable and responsive to those things that come along that are not quite expected. That is what makes this practice an art. It is an interaction between a caring and informed person trying to help another person in need of help. Compassion and humility smooth out the bumps along the road.

Can you pause at this point and call up the feelings of fear and dread you had about doing something clumsy in front of others? Can you remember being fearful that you would drop something or knock something over at a time when people will notice? It is rare when testing a student with ADHD that he does not knock his chair over, or drop test materials on the floor. This is the world of the individual with ADHD, constantly doing something that will elicit criticism or censure from those around him. As my grandfather often said, "Leave him alone, it's tough enough being a kid."

Now imagine these individuals going to schools where people wishing to be considered professionals vary widely in their sensitivity for people with ADHD. The very people that they are forced by mandatory attendance laws to be exposed to for six hours every day may be compounding their adjustment difficulties. Can you feel empathy for their vulnerability?

No individual teacher working with them needs to know everything there is to know about ADHD. They should not be expected to be expert at crafting varied intervention strategies. They should, however, be empathetic. They should have access to intervention teams within the school who will pool their combined experience to create a plan that will be helpful. In the meantime, they need to assure the student that they are there to help. They need to demonstrate an unfeigned sensitivity to the human being trapped inside all those annoying symptoms.

This quality of genuine caring is what makes all the difference in working with people at any level. True caring is inventive. As a culture, we seem to tolerate the inventiveness inspired by true caring differently from setting to setting. Nurses were expected to have it, but doctors were not. Internists were expected to have more of it, but surgeons were not. Tragically, it seemed like the more skilled or trained a person was, the less he was expected to have this inventive caring. It may have been related to what was called a "pecking order." I use the word "tragically" because this phenomenon has caused a lot of anger, resentment, and revenge in our society. We have paid a bitter price in our criminal justice system and beyond for tolerating a lack of caring in some sectors of our society.

Slowly, like the movement of a glacier, we see the value we place on the inventiveness inspired by true caring spread across all professions. Kindergarten teachers were expected to have it, but high school teachers were not. Then there was a movement toward "middle schools," which raised the importance of this inventiveness of genuine caring in the professionals working with our children in junior high schools. There was a view that teachers in younger grades taught the student, and teachers in high schools taught the subject.

This emphasis on the inventiveness of genuine caring is now moving into high schools as well. As our prison population passes 3%, perhaps we are awakening to an awareness that we can no longer afford to ride roughshod over people with individual differences in learning needs. We must care for each and every one and be as inventive as possible to help all achieve their personally defined levels of excellence over and over again.

The ADHD population represents one large group who has been mistreated all too often by institutions forced into a mass production mentality by funding that was all too scarce. I am left numb from the shock of learning that we as a society are paying $36,000 a year for a prison inmate. At the same time the average community is paying $3,600 a year per pupil on educational programming with the global, unfocused wish of keeping them out of prison, and making them productive tax payers.

This book hopes to make it clear that the contrast of productive tax payers versus prisoners is far too crude a focus. There are millions of people with significant learning challenges that make life hostile and frustrating for them. They are not realizing their full potential, and we all suffer when these individuals fail to realize their full potential.

We may be able to live without the benefits of these fully realized potentials—but do we have a responsibility of using what we know to ensure the full and healthy development of everyone? We have shown increasing sensitivity to individuals with other challenges and poured resources into their full and healthy development. We have done so from a belief that we, as a developed society, owe it to them. We have been surprised to learn that we have benefited greatly from this seemingly charitable effort.

There is every reason to believe that the ADHD population would be one of the richer fields to harvest in this same way.

References

Abikoff, H. (1991). Cognitive training in ADHD children: Less to it than meets the eye. *Journal of Learning Disabilities, 24,* 205-209.

American Academy of Pediatrics. (1987). Medication for children with attention-deficit disorder. *Pediatrics, 80,* 758-760.

American Psychiatric Association. (1994). *Diagnostic and statistical manual of mental disorders* (4th ed.). Washington, DC: Author.

Anastopoulos, A. D., & Costabile, A. A. (1995). The Conners' Continuous Performance Test: A preliminary examination of its diagnostic utility. *ADHD Report, 3,* 7-8.

Anderson, J., Williams, S., McGee, R., & Silva, P. (1989). Cognitive and social correlates of DSM-III disorders in preadolescent children. *Journal of the American Academy of Child and Adolescent Psychiatry, 28,* 842-846.

Anhalt, K., McNeil C. B., & Bahl, A. B. (1998). The ADHD classroom kit: A whole-classroom approach for managing disruptive behavior. *Psychology in the Schools, 35,* 67-79.

Balthazor, M. J., Wagner, R. K., & Pelham, W. E. (1991). The specificity of the effect of stimulant medication on classroom learning-related measures of cognitive processing for attention deficit disorder children. *Journal of Abnormal Child Psychology, 19,* 35-52.

Barkley, R. A. (1994). Editor's note. *ADHD Report, 2,* 3.

Barkley, R. A. (1997a). Editor's note. *ADHD Report, 5,* 16.

Barkley, R. A. (1997b). Update on a theory of ADHD and its clinical implications. *ADHD Report, 5,* 10-13.

Barkley, R. A. (1997c). *Defiant children: A clinician's manual for assessment and parent training* (2nd ed.). New York: Guilford Press.

Barkley, R. A., Fischer, M., Edelbrock, C. S., & Smallish, L. (1990). The adolescent outcome of hyperactive children diagnoses by research criteria. I. An 8-year prospective follow-up study. *Journal of the American Academy of Child and Adolescent Psychiatry, 29,* 546-557.

Biederman, J., Wilens, T., Mick, E., Faraone, S. V., Weber, W., Curtis, S., Thornes, A., Pfister, T., Jetton, J. G., & Soriano, J. (1997). Is ADHD a risk factor for psychoactive substance use disorder? Findings from a four-year prospective follow-up study. *Journal of the American Academy of Child and Adolescent Psychiatry, 36,* 21-29.

Bramlett, R. K., Nelson, P. & Reeves, B. (1997). Stimulant treatment of elementary school children: Implications for school counselors. *Elementary School Guidance and Counseling, 31,* 243-250.

Brooks, R. (1994). Enhancing self-esteem in children and adolescents with ADHD. *ADHD Report, 2,* 8-9.

Brooks, R. B. (1994). Children at risk: Fostering resilience and hope. *American Journal of Orthopsychiatry, 64,* 545-552.

Bussing, R., Schuhmann, E., Belin, T. R., Widawski, M., & Perwien, A. R. (1998). Diagnostic utility of two commonly used ADHD screening measures among special education students. *Journal of the American Academy of Child and Adolescent Psychiatry, 37,* 74-82.

Carlson, C. L., Tamm, L., & Gaub, M. (1997). Gender differences in children with ADHD, ODD, and co-occuring ADHD/ODD identified in a school population. *Journal of the American Academy of Child and Adolescent Psychiatry, 36,* 1706-1714.

Castellanos, F. X., Giedd, J. N., Marsh, W. L., Hamburger, S. D., Vaituzis, A. C., Dickstein, D. P., Sarfatti, S. E., Vauss, Y. C., Snell, J. W., Pajapakse, J. C., & Rapoport, J. L. (1996). Quantitative brain magnetic resonance imaging in attention-deficit hyperactivity disorder. *Archives of General Psychiatry, 53,* 607-616.

Conners, C. K., Levin, E. D., Sparrow, E., Hinton, S. C., Erhardt, D., Meck, W. H., Rose, J. E., & March, J. (1996). Nicotine and attention in adult attention deficit hyperactivity disorder (ADHD). *Psychopharmacology Bulletin, 32*, 67-73.

Connor, D. F., Harrison, R. J., & Melloni, R. H. (1996). Aggression and psychopharmacology in clinically referred children and adolescents. *ADHD Report, 4*, 3-7.

Corkum, P., Tannock, R., & Moldofsky, H. (1998). Sleep disturbances in children with attention-deficit/hyperactivity disorder. *Journal of the American Academy of Child and Adolescent Psychiatry, 37*, 637-646.

DuPaul, G. J., & Eckert, T. L. (1997). The effects of school-based interventions for attention deficit hyperactivity disorder: A meta-analysis. *School Psychology Review, 26*, 5-27.

DuPaul, G. J., Eckert, T. L., & McGoey, K. E. (1997). Interventions for students with ADHD: One size does not fit all. *School Psychology Review, 26*, 369-381.

Edwards, G. (1995). Use of negative consequences in parent training. *ADHD Report, 3*, 13-14.

Filipek, P. A., Semrud-Clikeman, M., Steingard, R. J., Renshaw, P. F., Kennedy, D. N., & Biederman, J. (1997). Volumetric MRI analysis comparing subjects having attention-deficit hyperactivity disorder with normal controls. *Neurology, 48*, 589-601.

Fisher, M. (1997). Persistence of ADHD into adulthood: It depends on whom you ask. *ADHD Report, 5*, 8-10.

Gadow, K. D., Sverd, J., Sprafkin, J., Nolan, E. E., & Ezor, S. N. (1995). Efficacy of methylphenidate for attention-deficit hyperactivity disorder in children with tic disorder. *Archives of General Psychiatry, 52*, 444-454.

Goldstein, S. (1997). What I've learned from 25 years in the field of hyperactivity/ADHD. *ADHD Report, 5*, 4-6.

Halperin, J. M., Newcorn, J. H., Koda, V. H., Pick, L., McKay, K. E., & Knott, P. (1997). Noradrenergic mechanisms in ADHD children with and without reading disabilities: A replication and extension. *Journal of the American Academy of Child and Adolescent Psychiatry, 36*, 1688-1696.

Hinshaw, S. P. (1997). What role do parent-child interactions and parenting beliefs play in ADHD? *ADHD Report, 5,* 6-10.

Horner, B. R., & Scheibe, K. E. (1997). Prevalence and implications of attention-deficit hyperactivity disorder among adolescents in treatment for substance abuse. *Journal of the American Academy of Child and Adolescent Psychiatry, 36,* 30-36.

Hoover, D. W., & Milich, R. (1994). Effects of sugar ingestion expectancies of mother-child interactions. *Journal of Abnormal Child Psychology, 22,* 501-515.

Jensen, P. S., Mrazek, D., Knapp, P. K., Steinberg, L., Pfeffer, C., Schowalter, J. & Shapiro, T. (1997). Evolution and revolution in child psychiatry: ADHD as a disorder of adaptation. *Journal of the American Academy of Child and Adolescent Psychiatry, 36,* 1672-1679.

Kent, J. D., Blader, J. C., Koplewicz, H. S., Abikoff, H., & Foley, C. A. (1995). Effects of late-afternoon methylphenidate administration on behavior and sleep in attention-deficit hyperactivity disorder. *Pediatrics, 96,* 320-325.

Levy, F. (1994). Invited guest editorial. Neurometrics: Review and Comments. *ADHD Review, 2,* 1-3.

Mannuzza, S., Klein, R. G., Bessler, A., Mallow, P., & LaPadula, M. (1993). Adult outcome of hyperactive boys educational achievement, occupational rank, and psychiatric status. *Archives of General Psychiatry, 50,* 565-576.

McMurray, M. (1995). Medication trials for children with ADHD. *ADHD Report, 3,* 11-12.

Merrell, K. W., & Wolfe, T. M. (1998). The relationship of teacher-related social skills deficits and ADHD characteristics among kindergarten-age children. *Psychology in the Schools, 35,* 101-109.

Milberger, S., Biederman, J., Faraone, S. V., Chen, L., & Jones J. (1997). ADHD is associated with early initiation of cigarette smoking in children and adolescents. *Journal of the American Academy of Child and Adolescent Psychiatry, 36,* 37-44.

Murphy, K. (1994). Guarding against overdiagnosis of ADHD in adults. *ADHD Report, 2,* 3-4.

Quay, H. C. (1997). Inhibition and attention deficit hyperactivity disorder. *Journal of Abnormal Child Psychology, 25*, 7-13.

Rapport, M. D., & Denney, C. (1997). Titrating methylphenidate in children with attention-deficit/hyperactivity disorder: Is body mass predictive of clinical response? *Journal of the American Academy of Child and Adolescent Psychiatry, 36*, 523-530.

Rapport, M. D., Denney, C., DuPaul, G. J., & Gardner, M. J. (1994). Attention deficit disorder and methylphenidate: Normalization rates, clinical effectiveness, and response prediction in 76 children. *Journal of the American Academy of Child and Adolescent Psychiatry, 33*, 882-893.

Ratley, J. J., Hallowell, E., & Miller, A. (1997). Psychosocial issues and psychotherapy in adults with attention-deficit disorder. *Psychiatric Annals, 27*, 582-586.

Richter-Sand, K. A. (1995). The impact of ADD on families and school relationships. *ADHD Report, 3*, 8-11.

Richters, J. E., Arnold, L. E., Jensen, P. S., Abikoff, H., Conners, K., Greenhill, L. L., Hechtman, L., Hinshaw, S. P., Pelham, W. E., & Swanson, J. M. (1995). NIMH collaborative multiside multimodal treatment study of children with ADHD: I. Background and rationale. *Journal of the American Academy of Child and Adolescent Psychiatry, 34*, 987-1000.

Romeo, V. (1996). Prevalence of childhood conduct and attention-deficit hyperactivity disorder in adult maximum security inmates. *International Journal of Offender Therapy and Comparative Criminology, 40*, 263-271.

Roy-Byrne, P., Scheele, L., Brinkley, J., Ward, N., Wiatrak, C., Russo, J., Townes, B., & Varley, C. (1997). Adult attention-deficit hyperactivity disorder: Assessment guidelines based on clinical presentation to a specific clinic. *Comprehensive Psychiatry, 38*, 133-140.

Sabian, B. (1995). Enhancing self-esteem and social skills in children with ADHD. *ADHD Report, 3*, 8-10.

Satterfield, J. S., & Schell, A. (1997). A prospective study of hyperactive boys with conduct problems and normal boys: Adolescent and adult criminality. *Journal of the American Academy of Child and Adolescent Psychiatry, 36*, 1726-1735.

Shapiro, E. S. (1995). A self-management technique for improving class-room behavior of students with ADD. *ADHD Report, 3*, 9-10.

Sieg, K. G., Gaffney, G. R., Preston, D. F., & Hellings, J. A. (1995). SPECT brain imaging abnormalities in attention deficit hyperactivity disorder. *Clinical Nuclear Medicine, 20*, 55-60.

Slomkowski, C., Klein, R. G., & Mannuzza, S. (1995). Is self-esteem an important outcome in hyperactive children? *Journal of Abnormal Child Psychology, 23*, 303-315.

Spencer, T. J., Biederman, J., Harding, M., O'Donnell, D., & Faraone, S. V. (1996). Growth deficits in ADHD children revisited: Evidence for disorder-associated growth delays? *Journal of the American Academy of Child and Adolescent Psychiatry, 35*, 1460-1469.

Stolowitz, M. (1997). Growing up with a non-visible disability. *ADHD Report, 5*, 9-11.

Swanson, J. M., Wigal, S., Greenhill, L. L., Browne, R., Waslik, B., Lerner, M., Williams, L., Flynn, D., Agler, D., Crowley, K., Fineberg, E., Baren, M., & Cantwell, D. P. (1998a). Analog classroom assessment of Adderall in children with ADHD. *Journal of the American Academy of Child and Adolescent Psychiatry, 37*, 519-526.

Swanson, J., Wigal, S., Greenhill, L., Browne, R., Waslik, B., Lerner, M., Williams, L., Flynn, D., Agler, D., Crowley, K. L., Pharm, D., Fineberg, E., Regino, R., Baren, M., & Cantwell, D. (1998b). Objective and subjective measures of the pharmacodynamic effects of Adderall in the treatment of children with ADHD in a controlled laboratory classroom setting. *Psychopharmacology Bulletin, 34*, 55-60.

Tannock, R. (1997). Television, video games, and ADHD: Challenging a popular belief. *ADHD Report, 5*, 3-7.

Wender, P. (1997). Attention deficit hyperactivity disorder in adults: A wide view of a widespread condition. *Psychiatric Annals, 27*, 556-561.

Wilens, T. E., Biederman, J., Mick, E., Faraone, S. V., & Spencer, T. (1997). Attention deficit hyperactivity disorder (ADHD) is associated with early onset substance use disorders. *The Journal of Nervous and Mental Disease, 185*, 475-481.

Wodrich, D. L., & Kush, J. C. (1998). The effect of methylphenidate on teachers' behavioral ratings in specific school situations. *Psychology in the Schools, 35*, 81-88.

Wolraice, M. A., Wilson, D. B., & White, W. (1995). The effect of sugar on behavior or cognition in children. *Journal of the American Medical Association, 274*, 1617-1621.

Wolraich, M. L., Feurer, I. D., Hannah, J. N., Baumgaertel, A., & Pinnock, T. Y. (1998). Obtaining systematic teacher reports of disruptive behavior disorders utilizing DSM-IV. *Journal of Abnormal Child Psychology, 26*, 141-152.

Resources

ADD Warehouse, 300 N.W. 70th Avenue, Suite 102, Plantation, FL 33317; 800/233-9273; http://www.addwarehouse.com

ADHD Report. Guilford Publications, Inc., 72 Spring Street, New York, NY 10012.

Barkley, R. A. (1997). *ADHD and the nature of self-control*. New York: Guilford Press.

Barkley, R. A. (1998). *Attention deficit hyperactive disorder: A handbook for diagnosis and treatment* (2nd ed.). New York: Guilford Press.

Barkley, R. A. (1997). *Defiant children: A clinician's manual for assessment and parent training* (2nd ed.). New York: Guilford Press.

Children and Adults with Attention Deficit Disorder. (1992). *C.H.A.D.D. educators manual: An in-depth look at attention deficit disorders from an educational perspective*. Plantation, FL: Author.

Dinkmeyer, D., Sr., McKay, G. D., & Dinkmeyer, D., Jr. (1997). *The parent's handbook: Systematic training for effective parenting*. Circle Pines, MN: American Guidance Service.

Ellis, D. B. (1991). *Becoming a master student* (6th ed.). New York: Houghton Mifflin.

Flick, G. L. (1998). *ADD/ADHD behavior-change resource kit*. West Nyack, NY: The Center for Applied Research in Education.

Gordon, M. (1991). *ADHD/Hyperactivity: A consumer's guide.* Dewitt, NY: GSI Publications.

Hallowell, E. M., & Ratey, J. J. (1994) *Driven to distraction.* New York: Simon & Schuster.

McCarney, S. B. (1989). *The attention deficit disorders intervention manual.* Columbia, MO: Hawthorne Educational Services, Inc.

McCarney, S. B. (1990). *The parent's guide to attention deficit disorders.* Columbia, MO: Hawthorne Educational Services, Inc.

McNamara, B. E., & McNamara, F. J. (n.d.). *Keys to parenting a child with attention deficit disorder.* Haupaugge, NY: Barron's Educational Services, Inc.

Parker, H. (1988). *The ADD hyperactivity workbook for parents, teachers, and kids.* Plantation, FL: Impact Publications.

Parker, H. (1992). *The ADD hyperactivity handbook for schools.* Plantation, FL: Impact Publications.

Phelan, T. W. (1996). *All about attention deficit disorder symptoms, diagnosis, and treatment: Children and adults.* Glen Ellyn, IL: Child Management, Inc.

Rief, S. (1997). *The ADD/ADHD checklist: An easy reference for parents & teachers.* Englewood Cliffs, NJ: Prentice Hall.

Sudderth, D. B., & Kandel, J. (1997). *Adult ADD-The complete handbook: Everything you need to know about how to cope and live well with ADD/ADHD.* Rocklin, CA: Prima Publishing.

Taylor, J. F. (1994). *Helping your hyperactive/attention deficit child.* Rocklin, CA: Prima Publishing.

Taylor, M., & McClure, F. D. (1996). *The down & dirty guide to adult ADD.* DeWitt, NY: GSI Publications, Inc.

Wachtel, A., & Boyette, M. (1998). *The attention deficit answer book: The best medications and parenting strategies for your child.* New York: Penguin Group.

Warren, P., & Capeheart, J. (1995). *You & your A.D.D. child: How to understand and help kids with attention deficit disorder.* Nashville, TN: Thomas Nelson Publishers.

About the Author

Paul L. Weingartner, M.A., is Executive Director of the Weingartner Center for Educational Excellence in Mansfield, Ohio. He is licensed in Ohio as a School Psychologist working in both public and private practice, where he has diagnosed and treated children and adults with ADHD for 16 years. (Mr. Weingartner has been diagnosed with ADHD, and knows the disorder from both sides of the clinical desk.)

He has written a weekly column, hosted a weekly call-in radio program on parenting, and conducted numerous workshops on ADHD and parenting. He serves on the School Psychology licensure examination committee for the Ohio Board of Psychology and on the executive board of the Ohio School Psychologists Association.

Mr. Weingartner received his B.A. in Elementary Education from The Ohio State University and his M.A. in Educational Psychology from Teachers College at Columbia University. He has also earned additional hours in School Psychology from The University of Akron and in Educational Administration from Bowling Green State University. He and his wife Adele have been married for 25 years and have three sons: Eric, Nicholas, and Ryan.

That's My Child: Strategies for Parents of Children with Disabilities
Lizanne Capper

This book explores the different sources of support available to parents with children who have all types of disabilities: a formal component (school systems, physicians, therapists, and support organizations) and an informal component (other parents of special-needs children, friends, family, and others) all sharing one common goal—wanting the best for the child.

That's My Child includes discussions of rights and referrals under federal law, school systems, special education, recreational activities, day care providers, and sections on families and friends.

To Order: 1996/0-87868-595-2   Stock #5952 $12.95

Write: CWLA
         P.O. Box 2019
         Annapolis Junction, MD 20701
e-mail: cwla@pmds.com

Call: 800/407-6273
       301/617-7825

Fax: 301/206-9789

Please specify stock #5952. Bulk discount policy (not for resale): 10-49 copies 10%, 50-99 copies 20%, 100 or more copies 40%. Canadian and foreign orders must be prepaid in U.S. funds. MasterCard/Visa accepted.

Developmental Disabilities and Child Welfare

Developmental Disabilities and Child Welfare

Ronald C. Hughes &
Judith S. Rycus

Excerpted from the *Field Guide to Child Welfare*, this book reviews the developmental disabilities that are most commonly seen by child welfare workers: cerebral palsy, epilepsy, mental retardation, spina bifida, autism, attention-deficit/hyperactive disorder, learning disabilities, and fetal alcohol syndrome. It then discusses the services that are needed by children with developmental disabilities and their families and the role that the child welfare field plays in providing these services.

To Order: 1998/0-87868-734-3   Stock #7343 $12.95

Write:	CWLA	Call:	800/407-6273
	P.O. Box 2019		301/617-7825
	Annapolis Junction, MD 20701		
e-mail:	cwla@pmds.com	Fax:	301/206-9789

Please specify stock #7343. Bulk discount policy (not for resale): 10-49 copies 10%, 50-99 copies 20%, 100 or more copies 40%. Canadian and foreign orders must be prepaid in U.S. funds. MasterCard/Visa accepted.

Helping Children Manage Stress: A Guide for Adults
James H. Humphrey

Helping Children Manage Stress clearly and carefully explains what adults can do to prevent and minimize the harmful consequences of stress in children. The first section reviews the general causes of stress, with particular emphasis on problems that originate at home and at school. The second part of the book provides standard stress reduction techniques that adults can use with children, such as the "relaxation response," meditation, progressive muscular relaxation, and various types of biofeedback, as well as a novel approach to use at the elementary school level: "story games." These games, presented in the form of a story that can be read to a group of children, are designed to engage them in a fun activity, and usually involve tension-relaxation exercises.

To Order: 1998/0-87868-668-1   Stock #6681 $18.95

Write:	CWLA	Call:	800/407-6273
	P.O. Box 2019		301/617-7825
	Annapolis Junction, MD 20701		
e-mail:	cwla@pmds.com	Fax:	301/206-9789

Please specify stock #6681. Bulk discount policy (not for resale): 10-49 copies 10%, 50-99 copies 20%, 100 or more copies 40%. Canadian and foreign orders must be prepaid in U.S. funds. MasterCard/Visa accepted.